# Awesome Facts for Minecrafters

## The Unofficial Collection

### Incredible & Exciting Facts about the Video Game

Edgar Rommel

Edition 1.0A

Author:
Edgar Rommel

Publisher:
Nucleo – a label of
my dna media GmbH
Ohmstr. 53
60486 Frankfurt am Main,
Germany

ISBN:
978-3-98561-061-7

**Feedback, Questions, Suggestions?**

Get in touch with us at **info@nucleo-media.com** or visit our homepage **nucleo-media.com**

On May 17, 2009, the time had finally come: Minecraft saw the light of day!

The Swede Markus Alexej Persson — better known by his stage name “Notch” — single-handedly released the first Java version, which at the time was only available for PC.

## Role Models

What do the video games *Dungeon Keeper, Infiniminer,* and *Dwarf Fortress* have in common? All three served as inspiration for the hit game *Minecraft*. Notch, the *Minecraft* inventor, loved the cave settings of the originals and wanted to develop a similar game. He added role-playing elements to the formula to round off the experience. The trick worked perfectly and is the reason for *Minecraft's* charm and success.

## "1% Sugar!"

"Bees, bees, bees, bees!" Does this phrase sound familiar? If so, you may have noticed the yellow text on the *Minecraft* start screen. There are now well over 400 of these so-called splash texts, and more and more are being added with each new game update. They can be references to *Minecraft* itself ("Buckets of lava!") or to well-known things on the internet or pop culture ("Han shot first!" — a reference to *Star Wars*).

## A Little Effort

Samuel Åberg is responsible for the sound design in *Minecraft* and takes his job very seriously. He visited Northern Europe's oldest dolphinarium near Stockholm to record real dolphin sounds. For panda noises, he even went one step further and traveled all the way to Southern China. He then assigned all these sounds to the blocky, virtual animals.

## A Hard Bed

Do you know which version of *Minecraft* it is that you play? Since September 20, 2017, the so-called *Bedrock Edition* has been the standard for most platforms — as its name suggests, it's the foundation for most *Minecraft* versions on consoles or other devices. It is based on the mobile *Pocket Edition,* which was released in 2011 and reprogrammed from scratch. Its program code is completely different from the original *Java Edition,* which has existed since May 2009. Therefore, mods from the *Java* version are incompatible with the *Bedrock Edition* and vice versa. This is one of the reasons why many PC gamers still prefer the old *Java Edition* of *Minecraft.*

## The Minecraft Guy? Steve!

Turquoise shirt, denim jeans, brown hair — if you're thinking of *Minecraft's* main character Steve, you're right. You usually get the Steve skin if you don't choose your own look for your character. But did you know that in the beginning, the character was simply called "Character" and was referred to by the gaming community as "the *Minecraft* guy"? It was only when Notch was asked about the character in an interview that he revealed the name: Steve.

## Three Dimensions

*Minecraft's* game world consists of three dimensions: the Overworld, the Nether and the End. When you start a new game, you begin in the Overworld. You can then use portals to enter the Nether, often referred to as the underworld due to its gloomy surroundings and lakes of lava. The End is typically considered its opposite. Located in an endless void, it is often compared to outer space. There, you can defeat the Ender Dragon and complete the game. Well, at least the end credits will run down, and then you can continue playing normally.

## Let the Music Play

C418 is not a programming code, but the stage name of the German musician Daniel Rosenfeld. Notch contacted him via an internet forum when Rosenfeld was 20 years old and asked him to compose the music and sound effects for *Minecraft.* No sooner said than done! He contributed his work from 2009 to 2021. His iconic musical style is also well-received outside of *Minecraft*, as Rosenfeld was also hired to provide the music for the TV series *Beyond Stranger Things.*

## Worms on the Internet

What do the games *Wurm Online* and *Minecraft* have in common? Notch worked on both titles. The Swede was the developer of the online game from 2002 to 2007. Initially, *Wurm Online* was even released under the company name Mojang Specifications. When Notch left the project, he took the studio's name with him — and today, Mojang is best known for *Minecraft.*

## Steve and Alex, Human Friends

Steve is clearly a boy — right? Although the main character has a male name, he is genderless, according to creator Notch. *Minecraft* is designed so that all living creatures in the game have both male and female characteristics, so animals of the same species can always mate. Notch has repeatedly emphasized that Steve is not a boy; Steve is a human. Nevertheless, an alternative skin, Alex, was made available in August 2014. It is particularly popular with female players thanks to its more feminine appearance. Of course, just like Steve, Alex is genderless and simply human.

## A Rapid Rise

When Jens "Jeb" Bergensten was hired as a temp at developer studio Mojang in December 2010, he probably had no idea that he would soon become the lead developer behind *Minecraft*. After the full version of the game was released just under a year later, Notch stepped back from further development. Instead, Jeb took over as lead developer of *Minecraft* in December 2011.

# Short & Sweet

*Minecraft* has not always been *Minecraft*. The first prototype of the game was called *Cave Game* by Notch. The name *Minecraft* only came a few days later with the release of the first alpha version.

*Minecraft's* significance for gaming and pop culture is enormous. It has been named the most influential video game of the 2010s by several renowned magazines, such as Polygon, and was inducted into the World Video Game Hall of Fame in June 2020.

An average of three million players dive into the *Minecraft* adventure every day.

The entire *Minecraft* ending — poem and credits — lasts a whopping 20 minutes. You can skip everything at the touch of a button to save yourself time.

# Short & Sweet

Whereas in the first developer version, there were just two blocks — Grass Block and Cobblestone Block — in the current game you can use more than 150 different blocks.

Have you noticed it yet? Whether on the official website or social media platforms, the Creeper's face is usually used as the profile picture for the official *Minecraft* accounts.

In an early version of *Minecraft,* players named "Notch" who were defeated would drop an apple. However, this Easter Egg has since been removed.

You can choose from over 125 different languages in *Minecraft* — including artificial languages such as Klingon (known from *Star Trek*) or pirate language. Arrr!

## A Real Bargain

*Minecraft's* success made such waves that Xbox manufacturer Microsoft set its sights on the brand. At the end of 2014, the tech giant struck and bought *Minecraft* for 2.5 billion dollars. Notch and the other two shareholders, Jakob Porsér and Carl Manneh, left the project — at least not with empty pockets.

## Buy Your Own Adventure

Want to personalize your adventure a little? Then you've probably already had a look at the *Bedrock Edition's* marketplace. There, you can buy additional content such as skins, mods, or texture packs with Minecoins and activate them in your game — whether you are building blocks on a PC or a console. If you participate in the Minecraft affiliate program, you can even sell your own creations on the marketplace. Before the official marketplace was introduced, you could also purchase additional content for *Minecraft*. However, you had to pay for it with real money — not Minecoins.

## What a Service

*Minecraft Realms* lets you create your own server for you and your friends. Your world will continue to exist even when no one is online, so you are not dependent on each other. You can, therefore, work on your shared world independently. Unfortunately, there is a monthly fee for Realms and Realms Plus. Although the realms are an integral part of the game and every *Minecraft* gamer will be familiar with them, they were not part of *Minecraft* from the very beginning. Realms were introduced worldwide only in 2014.

## Better Together

Since September 20, 2017, you can easily play with your friends, regardless of their platform. On that day, the Better Together Update was released, introducing the so-called cross-play feature. Since then, it doesn't matter if any of you are playing on a console, a computer, or a smartphone because you'll still end up on the same server across platforms. At least if you are all using the *Bedrock Edition.*

## The Unloved Second Child

While *Minecraft* was really taking off, developer Mojang announced another project in March 2011. The card game *Scrolls* was supposed to bring multiplayer battles to your smartphone and PC, but its release in December 2014 was already a bumpy ride. Apple refused to distribute the game via its App Store, as you had to create an extra account before you could start playing. And just six months later, it was announced that *Scrolls* would receive no further content. Then, in June 2018, Mojang surprisingly announced that the game would be given a new name — *Caller's Bane* — and would be free to play with immediate effect. A small community of fans keeps the game alive on private servers as best as they can.

## A Long Time in the Coming

Almost two and a half years after releasing the first *Minecraft Alpha Edition,* the full version was finally launched on November 18, 2011. It was unveiled at the Minecon and brought with it a host of new features, such as the Hardcore Mode and the End.

## Strategy against Piglins

If you are being chased by Creepers, Skeletons, or Spiders, that's usually a cause for concern — not so in *Minecraft Legends*. In this action-strategy game, you control hordes of monsters to avert an impending Piglin invasion from the Nether. It was an exciting premise, but not everyone took to the game when it was released in April 2023. While the Multiplayer Mode, which has always been important for all *Minecraft* games, was praised across the board, not everyone was happy with how elements of the strategy genre had been simplified. Perhaps this is why developer studio Mojang pulled the plug almost nine months later: In January 2024, it was announced that *Minecraft Legends* would no longer receive any new content. But don't worry. It's still playable.

## Hold Me Back

After Notch handed over his position as lead developer to Jeb, he stopped playing *Minecraft*. Why? The temptation to shower Jeb with suggestions for improvements would have been too great. As a result, he has turned to other games in his private life — such as the team shooter *Team Fortress 2*.

The first version of Minecraft was programmed in just six days.

Notch even completed the hardest part in a single weekend.

## Cave Exploration with a Difference

Did it feel like a major change to you, too? The *Minecraft Dungeons* game was released in May 2020, and has a completely different focus to the basic version of *Minecraft*. As the name suggests, the focus is not on building or crafting items, but on exploring caves and fighting. You can set off on an adventure with up to three friends and free the villagers from slavery. Also unusual: You don't watch your surroundings from a first-person perspective, but from a bird's eye view. Originally, the game concept was only intended as a single-player game for the Nintendo 3DS. However, the developers apparently liked the basic concept of *Minecraft Dungeons* so much that they expanded it and released it on several platforms — ironically, *Minecraft Dungeons* did not make it to Nintendo 3DS.

## What an Exciting Story

A serialized video game? *Minecraft Story Mode* was exactly that. The emphasis is on "was", as the game is unfortunately no longer available to buy since developer Telltale Games went bankrupt in 2018. The game, which consists of two episodic seasons, has you solving puzzles and making decisions in a typical point-and-click adventure style to advance the story of Jesse and his band of adventurers. *Minecraft Story Mode* was also released as an interactive TV series on Netflix but was removed from the platform in 2022.

## Divine Praise

Have you reached the End and defeated the Ender Dragon? Then, the nine-minute game credits begin to run: a poem of about 1,500 words. The dialog is probably between two god-like figures talking about you — the player — and your role in the universe. The text has already inspired and moved many *Minecraft* players. It was written by Irish author Julian Gough. Notch asked him to write a final poem after numerous players had recommended Gough as an accomplished lyricist.

## Proud and Fearful

One of his biggest fans was Notch's father. He always supported Persson and expressed his pride. His father was not only a fan of Notch's work on *Minecraft* but also an avid gamer. The one thing he was never a fan of was the monsters in the game. After Persson had added them, it had become a little too scary for his senior. It was probably the only criticism his father ever had of *Minecraft*.

## A Brief Pleasure

When graphic designer Hayden "Dock" Scott-Baron was hired as the first employee at Mojang in December 2009, the game characters in *Minecraft* looked completely different for about three months. Dock designed new 3D models that were much more complex than the blocky figures still used today. But even though Notch really liked the alternative models, he pulled the ripcord in February 2010 — adding the new characters to the game was much more complicated and time-consuming than initially expected. Dock, therefore, had to leave the project, and his creations, such as the female character "Rana" or the zombie-like "Beast Boy" were removed.

## No Power to the Griefers

Adventures without mining blocks? That sounds like *Minecraft's* Adventure Mode. This is designed specifically for Multiplayer Modes. You can still craft, but there are other limitations. For example, the administrator can define certain areas where building is possible or impossible. This allows player-created content or game concepts to be experienced. It also prevents griefing — the deliberate destruction of other players' buildings and all other forms of vandalism and misconduct — which unfortunately can sometimes occur on multiplayer servers. Incidentally, the term "griefing" was not coined by the *Minecraft* community but has been around since the 1990s, when the first online video games saw the light of day.

TNT

## Cry for Help?

Zombie Villagers are, as the name suggests, zombified Villagers. Their call is created by playing the calls of Villagers and Zombies at the same time. This sound is also slightly distorted. You can use a Golden Apple or special Splash Potions to turn Villagers back and save them.

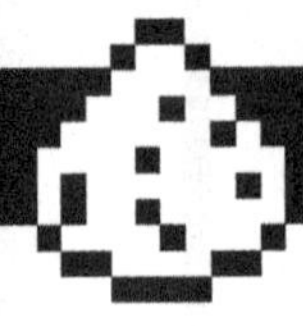

## Red Wonder Dust

Redstone Dust can be used to implement the wildest building concepts, as the material is conductive. This means that you can build circuits and thus functional devices. This can range from a simple doorbell to a fully automated forge. Some players go as far as building functioning calculators into *Minecraft.* Others go even further and build entire programs such as Gameboy emulators — so you can even play a game within a game. The sky's the limit with Redstone!

## Making School Fun

Have you ever used *Minecraft* at school? A teacher in the US was so enthusiastic about the game that he came up with the idea of using *Minecraft* in his classroom in early 2011. After all, various scenes can be recreated, and exciting experiments can be carried out with the conductive Redstone. His idea caught the attention of other teachers around the world, and the *MinecraftEdu* modification was created in the same year. In 2016, Microsoft bought the project, and *Minecraft Education* was born. It's that easy to move the classroom into the virtual world.

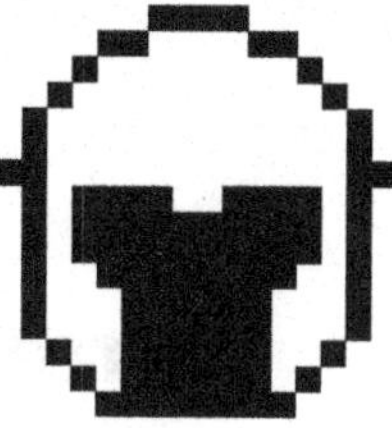

## Be Creative

Build to your heart's desire: This is exactly what Creative Mode is all about. It provides access to an unlimited number of blocks. This allows you to implement the craziest building projects — from colorful works of art to intricate Redstone constructions. There are virtually no limits to your creativity. You can also easily fly and dismantle blocks with a single touch, making it much quicker and easier to implement your ideas. Plus, you are invincible — unless you fall into the Void. Even if you do, you simply spawn again and can continue to express your creativity. Although Creative Mode was one of the first game modes in *Minecraft*, it has been removed and reinstated several times. With the Adventure Update, it finally became an integral part of *Minecraft* — along with the Survival Mode.

## Free Advertising

Do you remember how you found out about *Minecraft*? A 2011 study by the University of Southern California found that a third of players discovered *Minecraft* through the video-sharing site Youtube. Another third heard about the game from friends.

## Professional Player

In May 2023, Norwegian soccer star Erling Haaland broke the English league's goalscoring record and wanted to celebrate modestly with a round of gaming. But he couldn't reveal what he was playing. "It's too embarrassing!" he said. Some time later, he did reveal it in a podcast: Haaland doesn't kick virtual balls, he rather breaks down blocks in *Minecraft*. Preferably with his friends from home in Norway, of course.

## Just a Happy Accident

Does the Creeper creep you out? When Notch wanted to add a pig to the game, he accidentally swapped the values for height and length. The result was an elongated creature that stalks and stares at the player. As he found the non-pig creepy, Notch simply called his creation "Creeper" for obvious reasons. As if staring wasn't scary enough, he also gave the monster an explosive mind. Notch simply chose a leaf texture for the green skin color and gave it a face. And so, the Creeper was born.

# Short & Sweet

Do your parents ever use a gamepad? 11% of parents play *Minecraft* together with their children.

Many *Minecraft* enthusiasts also watch other players build blocks on the livestream platform Twitch. In August 2022, the category on Twitch had an average of 123,000 active viewers — a record for *Minecraft*.

Fancy a sequel? In December 2022, Notch revealed on the platform X that he is constantly being asked about *Minecraft 2.* He stated that he finds *Minecraft*$^3$ more interesting — an admittedly bad pun — alluding to the cube-shaped blocks.

With around 186 million active players as of November 2023, *Minecraft* has set an impressive record number.

## Short & Sweet

After *Minecraft* inventor Notch made several racist and trans-hostile comments on the internet, Microsoft removed all mentions of Notch and references to him via an update in 2019.

In keeping with the Halloween season, bats spawn more frequently than usual — at least in the *Java Edition.*

Nowadays, you can just go to the store and buy *Minecraft.* But in the early years of the game, things were very different. Back then, you could only download *Minecraft* from the official website.

Every Mojang employee who stayed with the company for six months after *Microsoft's* takeover in November 2014 received a bonus payment of around 300,000 dollars.

## Sticking Together

You've probably already built blocks together with your friends. *Minecraft* is known for its multiplayer fun, and the developers at Mojang Studios know this, too. That's why all games in the series — *Minecraft Legends* or the original — always include Cross-Play Multiplayer. This means you can play together with your friends online, whether they are on a PC, Nintendo Switch, or Playstation.

## What Is a Chunk?

16 by 16 by 384 blocks — that's the size of the area that makes up a so-called chunk. This part of the *Minecraft* world is only loaded when you get close to it. This prevents the entire *Minecraft* world from loading at once — that would probably take up a lot of time and processing power on your gaming device. The *Java Edition* for 64-bit devices typically has 625 chunks (12 per direction). In the *Bedrock Edition,* there are usually between 169 chunks (6 per direction) and 1089 chunks (16 per direction), depending on the platform.

## Make It Micro

*Minecraft* and Lego — already at first glance, it seems like a perfect match. That's why the two brands have been working together for some time. In 2012, the first *Minecraft*-themed Lego set was released in the Micro World series. As the name suggests, you could use it to recreate the blocky worlds in micro-format. *Minecraft* Lego sets in normal size have only been available since 2014. By the way, 90% of the proceeds from the Micro World sets were donated.

## Chips or Fries?

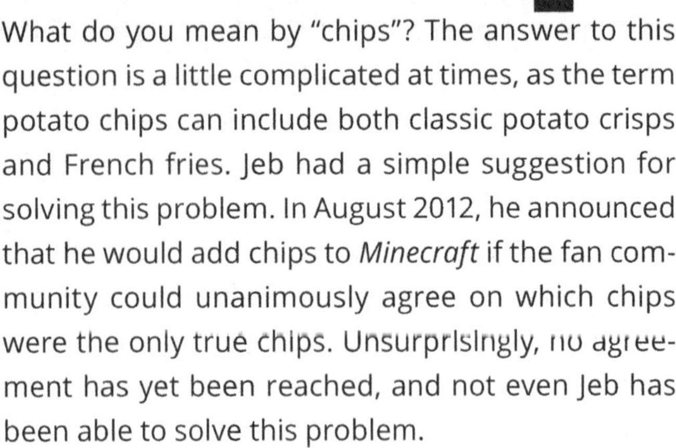

What do you mean by "chips"? The answer to this question is a little complicated at times, as the term potato chips can include both classic potato crisps and French fries. Jeb had a simple suggestion for solving this problem. In August 2012, he announced that he would add chips to *Minecraft* if the fan community could unanimously agree on which chips were the only true chips. Unsurprisingly, no agreement has yet been reached, and not even Jeb has been able to solve this problem.

## Minecraft Go — Maybe?

What a great gift: The *Minecraft Earth* smartphone app was announced in May 2019 to mark *Minecraft's* 10th anniversary. It allowed you to use your smartphone camera to capture your surroundings and build blocks in that projection — known as augmented reality (AR). Because of this feature, the game has often been compared to the smartphone hit *Pokémon Go.* Although an Early Access version of *Minecraft Earth* was launched in the fall of 2019, the project was officially scrapped in summer 2021. Microsoft cited the Covid pandemic as the reason.

## The End of Dimensions

Have you noticed that there are Endermen in all three dimensions? They are the only creatures to which this applies. And there's a simple but fatal reason for this: Endermen want to destroy all three dimensions once and for all. That's probably why they somehow manage to use portals and mine blocks so diligently. In this light, their name takes on a whole new meaning.

## Blocky Coming Together

Celebrating *Minecraft* with your friends in real life — is there anything better? Minecon made it possible. Between 2011 and 2016, the annual convention centered around everyone's favorite game took place first in Las Vegas and later in Anaheim. In the years that followed, there were numerous name changes and the leap to a livestream event. As of 2020, the event is simply called *Minecraft Live*.

## Convenient Shortcut

Everyone in the *Minecraft* community understands "mob" to mean the same thing: creature. The term is short for "mobile entity." It has now also been officially adopted by Mojang and is used as a matter of course in *Minecraft,* from monsters in *Minecraft Story Mode* being called mobs to the character Farnum in the *Minecraft* novel *Return of the Piglins* talking about wanting to take care of rare mobs.

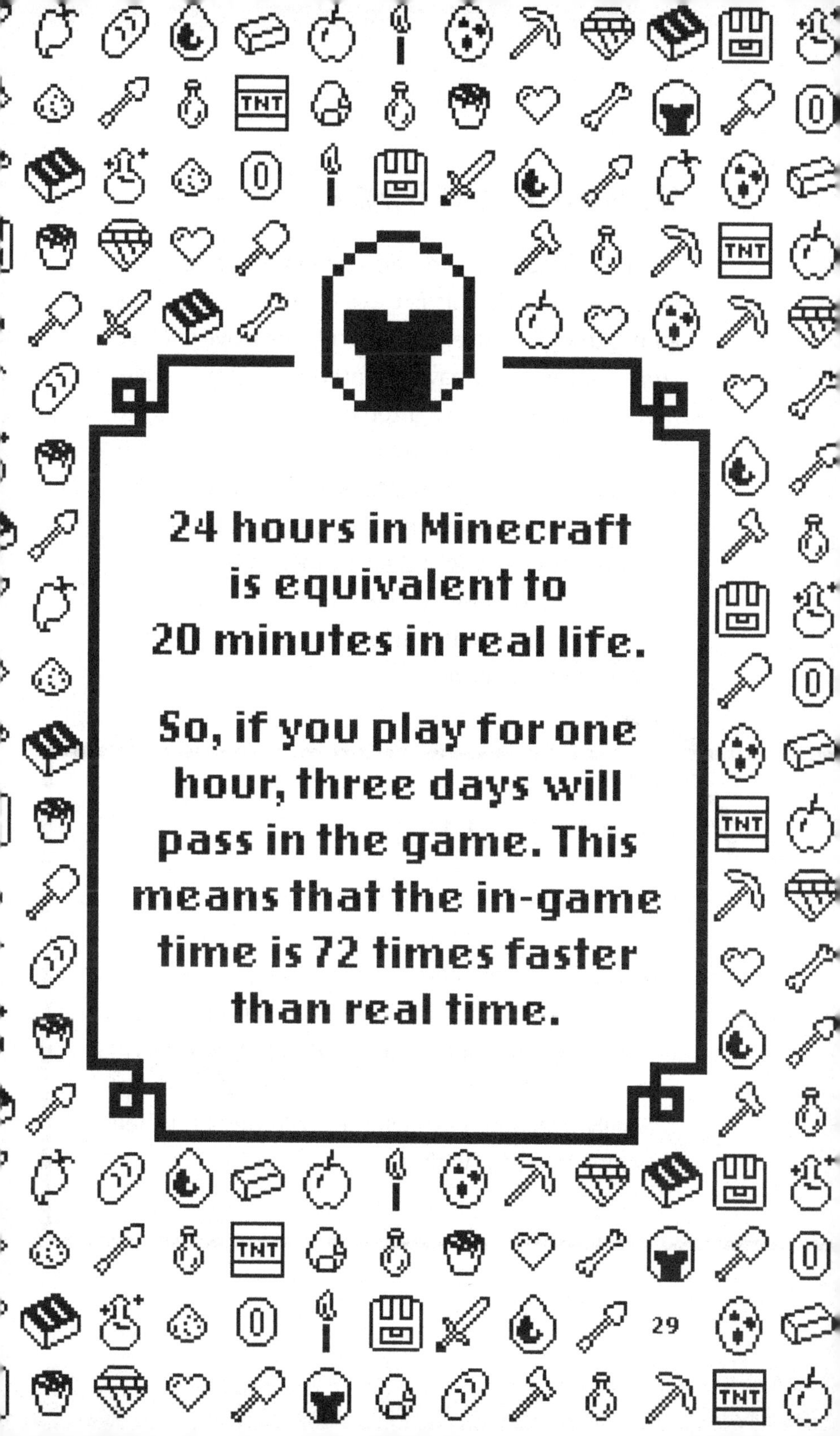

24 hours in Minecraft is equivalent to 20 minutes in real life.

So, if you play for one hour, three days will pass in the game. This means that the in-game time is 72 times faster than real time.

## Of Good and Bad Clones

If you have success, you also have imitators. In the case of *Minecraft,* this is clear from the number of games that have attempted to ride the wave of *Minecraft's* success and have adopted certain game elements. These titles are often disparagingly referred to as *Minecraft* clones by the gaming community. *Terraria,* on the other hand, is probably a positive example: The title was also released in 2011 and has already attracted more than 44 million buyers with its sandbox gameplay. The game has since been released on all major platforms. The big difference to *Minecraft*? *Terraria* has a 2D perspective.

### Empty Tool Belt

It's worth taking a closer look. A few tools can be seen on the side of the Crafting Table: a hammer, a saw, and a pair of pliers. There are also some other utensils on the Crafting Table. Even though there are now various tools in *Minecraft,* the tools shown on the Crafting Table and the Smithing Table are not officially available in the game. Will they find their way into *Minecraft* with future updates?

## A Long Lunge

When *Minecraft* characters Steve and Alex were announced as fighters for the video game *Super Smash Bros. Ultimate* in October 2020, there was a huge uproar in the gaming community. Fans around the world had long hoped that Steve would find his way into Nintendo's fighting game. Other characters, such as the Pig and the Creeper, are also included as costumes. According to former producer Daniel Kaplan, Mojang and Nintendo had been in talks to include Steve in the *Super Smash Bros.* series for at least five years.

## An Uncomfortable Pose

Are you riding or steering a boat and needing to check something in your inventory at the same time? You may have noticed that your character has a strange pose in the inventory menu. This is because your character remains aligned there as if riding a horse or driving a boat, without the mount or vehicle being visible. If you open your inventory while lying in bed, the same thing will happen.

## And Action!

*Minecraft* is a huge thing on Youtube! Just look at the numbers on the official channel: More than 12 million subscribers and over 850 videos speak for themselves. Apart from uploaded video announcements, there are funny clips about all the creatures in the *Minecraft* world.

## Construction Site Ahead

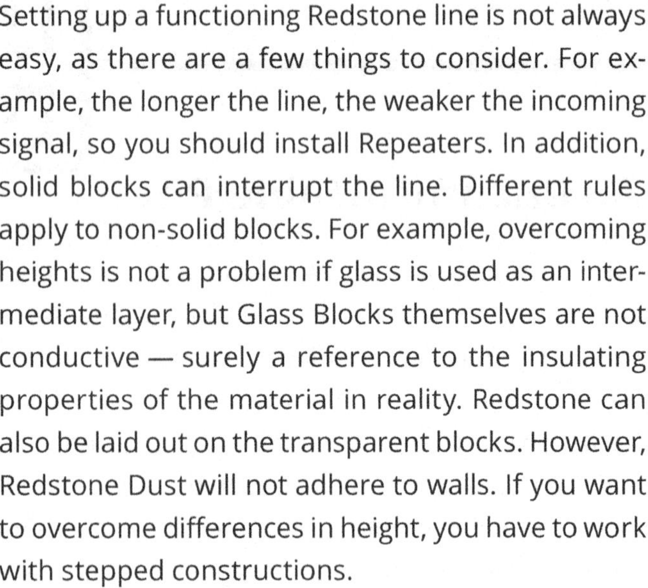

Setting up a functioning Redstone line is not always easy, as there are a few things to consider. For example, the longer the line, the weaker the incoming signal, so you should install Repeaters. In addition, solid blocks can interrupt the line. Different rules apply to non-solid blocks. For example, overcoming heights is not a problem if glass is used as an intermediate layer, but Glass Blocks themselves are not conductive — surely a reference to the insulating properties of the material in reality. Redstone can also be laid out on the transparent blocks. However, Redstone Dust will not adhere to walls. If you want to overcome differences in height, you have to work with stepped constructions.

# Short & Sweet

Baby Piglins will sometimes jump onto the backs of Baby Hoglins and ride them. However, if there are more Baby Piglins than mounts in the area, they will jump onto a rider's shoulder — allowing up to three of the little Piglins to ride a Baby Hoglin.

Trees can't fall over in *Minecraft*! Or can they? In the *Bedrock Edition,* fallen trees are generated occasionally, but this never happens in the *Java Edition.*

50% of all *Minecraft* players under the age of 12 say they love playing alone. Nevertheless, a whopping 80% regularly play multiplayer modes.

Since Microsoft acquired the rights to *Minecraft* in 2014, it has added around 250 million new players and generated around 2.8 billion dollars in revenue.

## Short & Sweet

Have you ever fallen for one of Mojang's April Fools' pranks? The *Minecraft* development studio comes up with a new gag every year. For example, on April 1, 2017, Mojang announced a fictitious *Minecraft* console, — but its technology was several decades out of date.

Thanks to the large number of different armor pieces, more than 212 billion different outfits are possible.

Meowing Ghasts? Sounds strange, but the calls of the Nether monsters are the modified meows of music producer C418's cat.

If you want to make a wolf your companion, you will need to feed it Bones. Each Bone has a one-in-three chance of the wolf becoming tame and following you.

## As You Like It

Have you ever tried a modified version of *Minecraft?* So-called mods are very popular in the community and make all kinds of things possible. One popular modification, for example, is the alternative Survival Mode *Skyblock*. In this mode, you start your adventure on a floating island, and you must make do with the very limited resources and craft new objects in order to progress. Mods are not unique to *Minecraft*, as most PC games are modified in one way or another by industrious hobbyists. Other popular titles in the modding community include games from the *GTA* or *The Elder Scrolls* series.

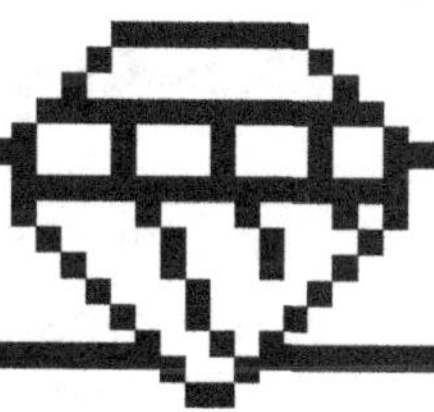

### Two for One

You want to play *Minecraft* on a PC platform but can't decide which version to play — *Java* or *Bedrock*? That's no problem, as both versions have been offered together since summer 2022. For example, if you buy the *Java Edition*, the *Minecraft Bedrock Edition* will automatically be added to your Microsoft account — and vice versa, of course.

## Everything Stays the Same

Chests are handy, aren't they? A normal Chest can hold 27 stacks, or 1,728 blocks in total, and a Large Chest can even double your storage space. But what's the difference to a Shulker Box, which you can craft from the remains of the monster Shulker found in the End? Although this cannot be enlarged, it retains its contents when it is dismantled — a normal Chest will drop its entire contents in such a case.

### The Sky Is the Limit

Islands in the sky — an exciting idea, isn't it? This is exactly what was planned for *Minecraft* back in 2011 when Mojang was working on a celestial dimension. This would be the counterpart to the subterranean Nether and be located above the clouds. Officially, this dimension was never added to the game, but you can use tricks and modifications to access these sky-islands. Ultimately, however, the idea for the sky dimension was scrapped, and the End was added instead — which also features flying islands.

## No Sharpener Necessary

Pistons are practical because they can move blocks via a Redstone circuit. And they gave the developer Jeb an idea — pointed blocks! Co-developer Dinnerbone also thought that the Tripwire could be used to build insidious traps if there were pointy-headed Pistons. In the end, however, the idea was probably too macabre, so pointed blocks never made it into the game.

## Not a Party

A huge *Minecraft* festival was planned for September 2020 in Florida — but the Covid pandemic put the work on hold. And even though the event was supposed to happen again, it hasn't yet. Instead, the *Minecraft Festival* has been canceled several times in the years since. At least Minecraft Live, the annual livestream event, can keep you entertained instead.

## Not So 3D

Although *Minecraft* is owned by Xbox manufacturer Microsoft, the game is also released on numerous other platforms, such as the Nintendo 3DS. *Minecraft — New Nintendo 3DS Edition* was launched on the US market in September 2017. Due to the technical challenges, you can only enjoy the game if you own a New Nintendo 3DS, 3DS XL, or 2DS XL. Unfortunately, devices that do not belong to the *New* series are incompatible. Also, the game cannot display the spatial 3D effect that Nintendo 3DS is known for.

## A Little Tight

Piglins were added to *Minecraft* in June 2020 with the Nether Update — and Mojang had to make a small adjustment. The heads of the monsters are wider than those of the player characters. To ensure that helmets would fit correctly in the future, the helmet model was modified specifically for the Piglins.

## Better Well-Ported than Poorly Developed

The original console versions of *Minecraft* were not ported to the Xbox 360 and Nintendo Switch by Mojang, but by 4J Studios. The developer studio is based in Scotland and is known for its ports — meaning the adaptation of the same game for different platforms. For example, the Playstation 3 version of *The Elder Scrolls 4 Oblivion* was penned by 4J Studios, as were the Xbox ports of the classic video games *Banjo-Kazooie* and *Banjo-Tooie*.

## Everything Revolves Around You

No matter where you are in the game world, you always remain the center of the world. This is because the sun and moon in *Minecraft* are not governed by astronomical rules but by you, the player. This is why phenomena such as a solar eclipse are not even possible. And theoretically, there should be a lunar eclipse every night — the phenomenon where the Earth comes between the sun and the moon and casts a shadow on the latter.

## The Pink King

*Minecraft* Youtuber Technoblade started uploading videos to the internet when he was just 14 years old. Alexander, as he is known by his real name, not only impressed with his player-versus-player skills but also dared to take on other challenges — such as playing through Hardcore Mode with a steering wheel controller.

Sadly, Technoblade fell ill with cancer and passed away in June 2022 at the age of 23. In his honor, a small change has been made to the *Minecraft* launcher, the program that starts *Minecraft* games on the PC: The pig featured on a graphic now wears a crown. This is based on Technoblade's logo, which also consists of a pig wearing a crown. At the time of his death, Technoblade had almost 11 million subscribers, but since then, around six million more have been added.

## Even a Helmet Won't Help

Blocks float in the air where they have been generated or placed — *Minecraft's* physics are obviously different from the physics of the real world. Nevertheless, gravity can also play a role in the game. Some blocks are affected by gravity and can be dangerous for you if they fall on you. Sand and gravel in particular have been known to bury careless players who are mining upwards.

## Strong Butt Muscles

With enough stamina, this world record can also be broken: On June 7, 2021, Frenchman Alexandre Jouniaux was awarded the Guinness World Record for the longest uninterrupted *Minecraft* session at 38 hours and 1 second. He had already started the attempt on June 5, beating the previous record holder by two hours. Other players and Youtubers have been posting their own (alleged) records online, surpassing Alexandre's number of hours. But nowadays, it is no longer difficult to fake such posts.

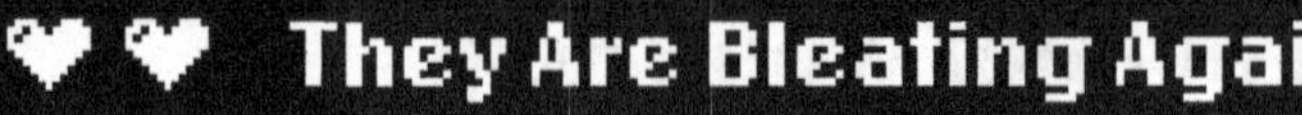

## They Are Bleating Again

Annoying or not, that's for you to decide: Goats in *Minecraft* have a two percent chance of being screaming goats. That means they make shrill calls. Although the animals are based on mountain goats, the sound designers at Mojang recorded the cries of domestic goats. They then mixed them with human calls and voilà — the goat cries are ready.

### A Picture Worth 1,000 Pixels

You can easily craft paintings with a block of Wool and eight Sticks. Depending on its placement on a wall, it automatically unfolds with a randomly selected image. Most of these paintings were painted by Notch's former brother-in-law Kristoffer Zetterstrand and then transferred to *Minecraft* as pixel graphics. Another painting, which is not based on a real image, shows the creation of a Wither. Jeb created it using a graphics program.

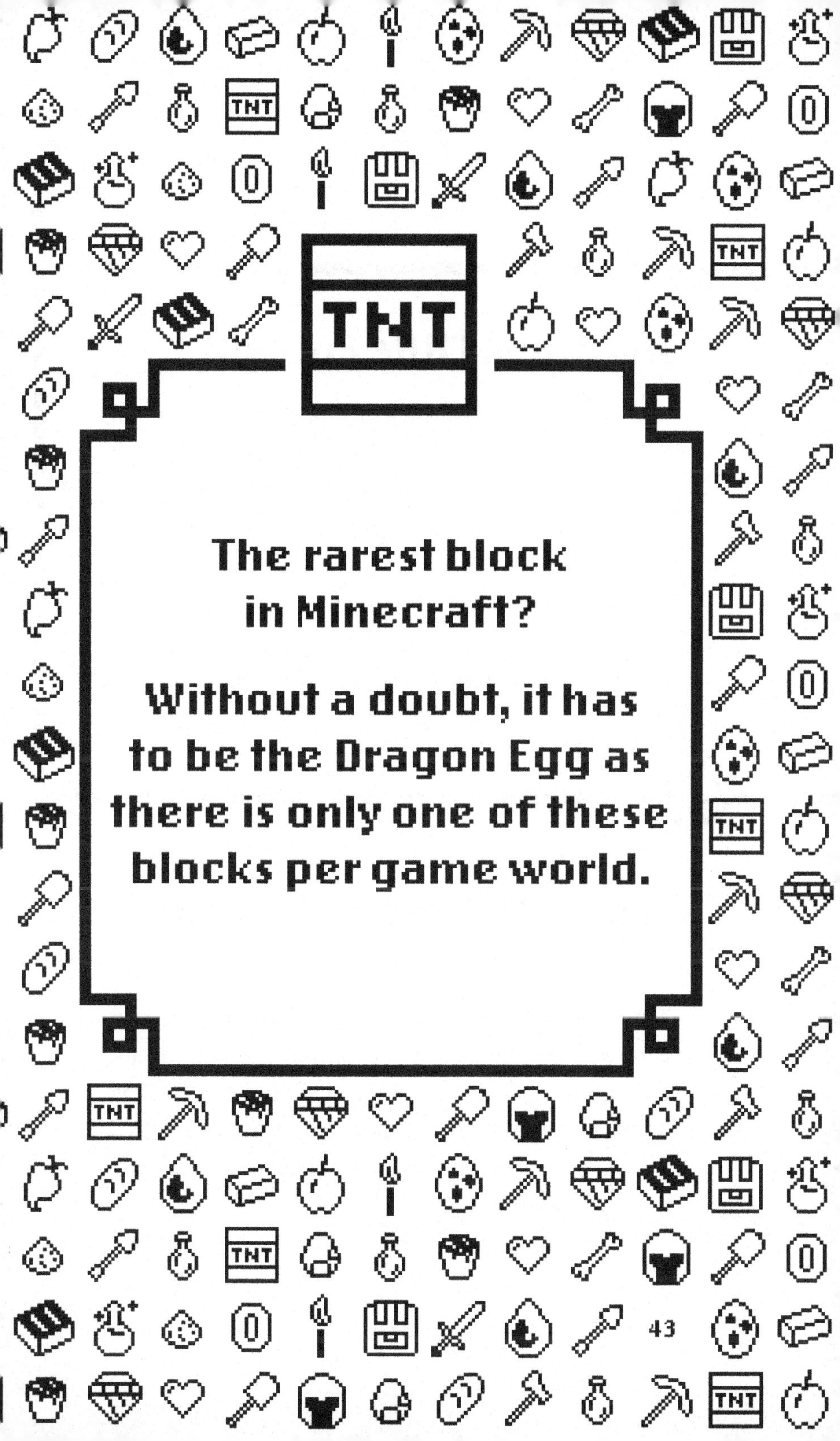


The rarest block in Minecraft?

Without a doubt, it has to be the Dragon Egg as there is only one of these blocks per game world.

## Big Brain, Little Content

The staff at Mojang have repeatedly brought up giant mobs as possible new creatures. One such monster is the Giant. At around 11 blocks tall, it is truly gigantic! It's a shame it didn't make it into the game as an official mob. In the *Minecraft Java Edition,* however, the Giant can be summoned with a command. However, as it has not been assigned an AI (artificial intelligence), it just stands around in the area.

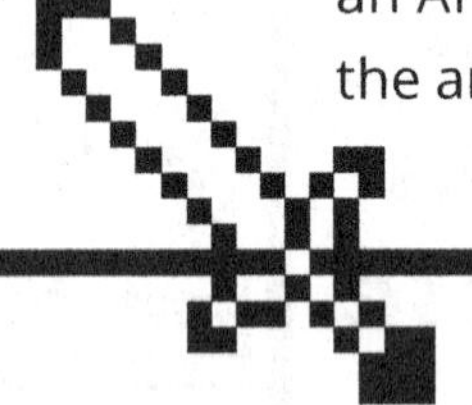

## Where Did You Come From, Where Did You Go?

Tadpoles grow into one of three different frog species — one species each in temperate, warm, and cold biomes. It doesn't matter where the tadpole hatches. What matters is the biome in which it grows up. You can collect and transport tadpoles using a bucket.

## Too Scary to Be True

Are you afraid of Herobrine? The eerie figure looks just like Steve — only with empty, white eyes. According to an internet legend, he appears in the fog, sets traps, lights things on fire, and stares at you from afar. Even though there are numerous eyewitness reports and photos of him, Herobrine is nothing more than a fantasy. He does not officially exist in any *Minecraft* game.

## White Medicine

Raid Captains are easily recognized by the banner they carry above their heads. Other Illagers will follow them and, if necessary, replace them as captain by picking up a dropped banner. If you are successful and kill a Raid Captain, you will receive the "Evil Doom" (*Bedrock Edition*) or "Impending Doom" (*Java Edition)* effect. This will automatically trigger a raid on a village as soon as you enter it. Can you reconcile this with your conscience? If not, just drink some milk — it will cancel the status effect.

## Killer Bees

If you attack bees, they will strike back. But if a mob attacks an industrious honey producer in the *Minecraft Java Edition,* it will be spared. However, this is completely different from the *Bedrock Edition.* Here, bees will stop at nothing to attack anyone and anything that harms them.

## Toxic Candy

In the past, if you wanted to tame a parrot, you had to feed it cookies. That's not a good idea, as one fan pointed out on Reddit. To make cookies in *Minecraft,* you need cocoa beans. But in the real world, these contain substances that are toxic to birds. So, if anyone had the idea to feed their feathered friend chocolate cookies, the poor animal could die. Mojang has responded to the feedback. Now, if you want to tame a parrot in *Minecraft,* you should use seeds. If you give the bird cookies instead, it will die. Splash texts have also been added to the start screen to warn against this type of feeding. Although there are no avocados in the game, a splash text also warns you about them: They also contain a substance poisonous to birds.

# Short & Sweet

Notch took the design of the leather armor from his unfinished game *Legend of the Chambered.* The same goes for the Apple and Sword mini icons.

Wardens will sniff you out and then attack relentlessly. As Mojang has revealed, they can smell and attack all creatures — but they will focus on the player if they are nearby.

Sometimes, bats are targeted by other mobs. But their completely wild flying behavior makes it difficult for anyone to hit them. So, a Wither on a bat hunt can devastate entire regions.

You can use dye to color not only wool but also the sheep itself. After shearing, she sheep will automatically turn white. There are 16 different colors in total, which can even be passed on.

## Short & Sweet

Say you manage to lure a Hoglin from the Nether to the Overworld or the End. In this case, the monster will turn into a Zombie after 15 seconds — this monster will then be called a Zoglin.

You can recognize an active Redstone line by the smoke particles and the red light it emits. But does it really produce its own light? It is more likely to be a glow, as the Redstone Line does not emit light in the dark.

In 2014, *Minecraft* creator Notch was considered one of Sweden's biggest taxpayers before emigrating to the US in December that year.

Just ride a pig — why not? Equip a pig with a saddle and use a carrot on a stick to control the pig.

## Early Practice

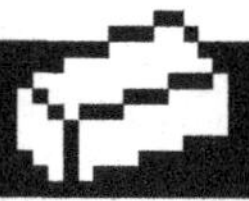

Jeb started learning programming languages such as Basic and Turbo Pascal at the age of 11 — and 10 years later, he was already making a name for himself as a map designer for the arena shooter *Quake 3.* His map "cpm4" became the most successful user map and was even used in the Euro Cup at the time.

## Oink

Once again, the idea came from the community: When pigs found their way into the game in an early version of *Minecraft*, player Miclee created a pig-man skin. His friend Xaphobia then created a zombified version of the skin in October 2010. Notch caught wind of this soon after and was so impressed with their creations that he officially added the zombie pig to the game for the upcoming Halloween holiday. The pig-man eventually became the monster Piglin, which was introduced to *Minecraft* in June 2020 with the Nether Update — almost 10 years later.

## Mini Minecraft

Programming a video game in just 48 hours? Notch did just that for a programming competition. The result is called *Minicraft* and looks like *Minecraft* meets parts of the early *The Legend of Zelda.* The game was released on December 19, 2011, and is still playable today. And although Notch announced a sequel in January 2012, it has not yet been released. Instead, Notch has published the project's source code to allow the fan community to continue modifying the game.

## Mind Your Steps

Have you ever wondered what the difference is between regular blocks of Ice and Packed Ice? Both behave relatively similarly and are naturally slippery, but there are some differences. For example, Packed Ice is not transparent because it is denser. If you craft nine blocks of ice together, you will get one block of Packed Ice. This density may also explain why it doesn't melt, even if you place Packed Ice near Lava or Fire.

## For a Good Cause

Buying games and doing some charity at the same time? If you buy from Humble Bundle, you can do just that. In 2012, Mojang and Humble Bundle teamed up for the charity event Mojam, and developed a 2D shooter called *Catacomb Snatch*. It sold 81,575 units and raised almost half a million dollars for a good cause. The project was revived over the next two years, with more mini-games sold — and, more importantly — more money raised.

0

## Not Just There

Have you always wanted to experience first-hand what it's like to mine blocks or be surprised by Creepers? Then check out *Minecraft's* Virtual Reality Mode! With the help of VR goggles, you can easily immerse yourself in the virtual world of blocks. Mojang has even optimized the controls and camera so that you don't get sick as quickly and can really enjoy the experience.

## Accidentally Cheated?

*Minecraft* Youtuber Dream made waves a few years ago, particularly with his speedrun videos. More than 31 million subscribers now follow his attempts to play *Minecraft* in record time. However, with so many viewers, inconsistencies are easier to spot — like in the spring of 2021, when doubts arose about the authenticity of Dream's records. Some statistics nerds then began their research, and indeed, the drop rate of Ender Pearls and Blaze Rods in Dream's streams was unusually high. Clay, as Dream is known by his real name, then spoke up again and apologized. He had accidentally left a modification activated that increases the drop rates of items important to progression through the game. True or not, his records are now officially invalid.

## Keep Your Word

Does the message "This message will never appear on the splash screen, isn't that weird?" sound familiar? Then you are definitely playing *Minecraft* in the *Bedrock Edition*. In the *Java* version, this message does not appear as a splash text in the start menu — so the *Java* version keeps its promise.

## A Little Help

You may know Mojang best as the developer studio of *Minecraft*. But did you know that the company also publishes games that it didn't program itself? Mojang has stepped in as publisher and co-publisher for the games *Cobalt* and *Cobalt WASD* from the Swedish developer Oxeye Game Studio.

## Serious Competition?

*Roblox* is often cited as one of *Minecraft's* biggest competitors. And there are indeed some parallels: minimalist graphics, active community involvement, and incredible record numbers. The difference, however, is that *Roblox* is a free-to-play title, meaning you don't have to buy it to play. Around three-quarters of all nine to 12-year-olds in the US now have a *Roblox* account. Not surprisingly, the number of users is enormous. As was the case in October 2021, when around 226 million players roamed the worlds of *Roblox*. By comparison, "only" around 173 million people played *Minecraft* in the same month.

## Barking Axolotl

What kind of sounds do the amphibian axolotls make? The sound designers at Mojang must have asked themselves the same question. The answer: Axolotls do not have vocal organs. However, as they breathe air, they do sometimes emit it noisily. Those responsible have painstakingly recorded these sounds and mixed them with the barking of dogs. This is how the axolotl sounds in *Minecraft* were created.

## The Uncensored Library

Press freedom is not established in some countries of the world — but *Minecraft* is often available there. That's why the organization Reporters Without Borders has set itself the task to build an in-game library of uncensored, freely accessible books and news — The Uncensored Library. The works are available in various languages and are regularly updated. And by the way, the library building also looks great.

## Even without Redstone

Note Blocks outside of *Minecraft*? With *Minecraft Note Block Studio,* you can compose your own songs on your PC based on the sounds of the Note Blocks in the game. All you need is a basic understanding of music. As the program is based on open-source code and is not officially distributed by Microsoft, it is free of charge in the true spirit of fan projects.

## You Only Had One Job

There are only enemies in the Nether — because the Nether is a dangerous place. One of its inhabitants is the Blaze, a smoldering creature made of pieces of lava. Apparently, it was created by the former inhabitants of the Nether fortresses as a guard, but instead of protecting them, it seems to have destroyed them. Jeb actually had the idea for the monsters long before he started working on *Minecraft*, as he originally designed them for his game *Whispers in Akarra.*

## Our Green Village

Cobblestone with moss — the result: Mossy Cobblestone. This block is perfect for creating an old or rundown look. Not surprisingly, the Mossy Cobblestone was once used as a decorative element for villages. In the *Minecraft Bedrock Edition* the block is used in this way, at least in Zombie Villages. In the *Java Edition,* however, the Zombie Villages can do without the special block.

## Tips for Gardening

Contrary to the rumor that trees in *Minecraft* can keep growing after a certain amount of time, they do not. Trees grow from a seedling to the size of — depending on the species — 4 to 16 blocks. However, this growth can also be destructive. For example, if there are torches where the tree's crown is developing, these objects will simply be destroyed. So be careful where you plant your seedlings.

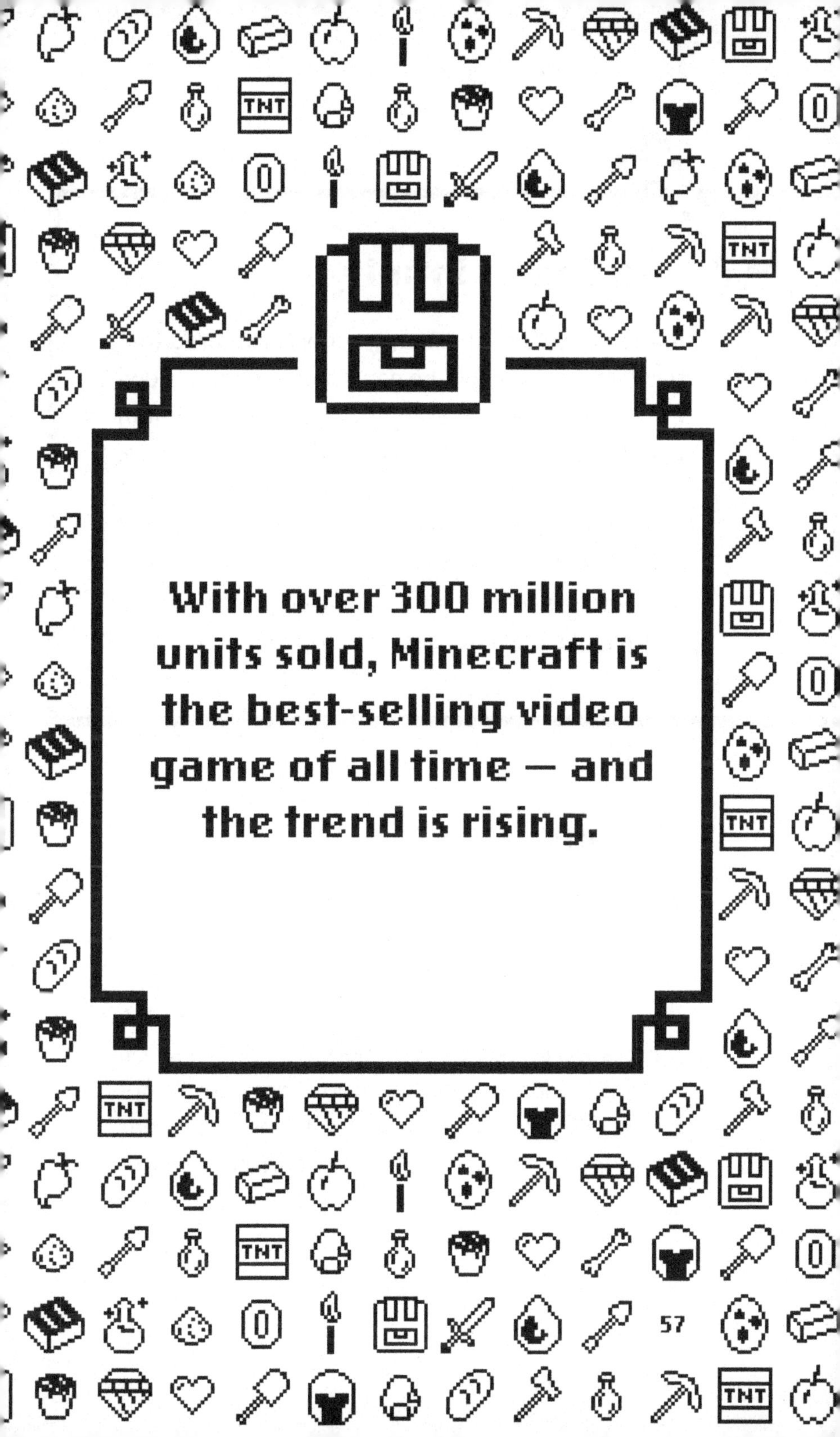

With over 300 million units sold, Minecraft is the best-selling video game of all time — and the trend is rising.

## The End of Infinity

In the early days of *Minecraft,* it was rumored that the game world could be generated infinitely. However, due to technical limitations, the maximum world size is now 30 million blocks in any direction. In earlier versions, it was possible to exceed this size, resulting in serious gameplay and graphics errors. If you travel to the end of the world today, you will come across a limit — the so-called World Barrier, which looks like a transparent striped curtain.

## Unsolicited Calls

What are parrots known for? They imitate you — you! And so even Creepers are not spared the teasing of their feathered companions. Although the explosive mobs don't have any distinctive calls, parrots will imitate the Creepers' hiss before an explosion. So don't be alarmed if you hear a suspicious hiss coming from your shoulder: It's not a Creeper. It's your naughty parrot. Naughty parrot.

## Three Day Birthday

Everyone should celebrate their 10th birthday — even a video game! When *Minecraft* completed its first decade on May 17, 2019, a "10" appeared on every cake in the game, as if it were a giant candle. The celebrations were accompanied by a splash text in the start menu that read "Turning 10 years old!" Three days later, the decorations were removed, and the party was over.

## Do Not Touch Your Face

With most of the world in quarantine during the Covid pandemic, many players rediscovered *Minecraft* — and Mojang must have felt a sense of responsibility. During this time, new splash texts were added to the start menu that referenced the pandemic. With slogans such as "Cough or sneeze into your elbow!" or "Gamers unite — separately in your own homes!" the Swedish developer wanted to remind you and your friends to take care of your health while playing.

## Digital Lego Blocks

Nowadays, everyone knows the Lego sets from *Minecraft*. But did you know that a Lego *Minecraft* video game was once planned? There were concrete plans in 2011, and developer Mojang even started work on the first prototype. The game was going to be just like *Minecraft* — but with the iconic Lego bricks. However, because Lego is very protective of its brand and has many guidelines for collaborations, the work became too complicated for Mojang, and the Swedish development studio ended the collaboration.

## Green Meadow

A block of dirt can turn into a block of grass if they are not far apart. Conversely, a block of grass will always turn into dirt when mined — unless you have cast the Silk Touch enchantment on one of your tools, such as the shovel. In this case, the block will be mined in its current form as a Grass Block. The only other way to get such a drop is a little more brutal: Kill an Enderman holding a Grass Block. He'll drop it, and you won't have to use the enchantment.

# Short & Sweet

Although you need four Stone Blocks to produce Stone Bricks, you get exactly four bricks — so you have no loss. However, it takes a little longer to mine Stone Bricks than it does to quarry normal stone.

Bored? Then try walking from Spawn Point Zero to the World Barrier. It will take about 140 days on foot — that's 20 weeks or almost five months.

*Minecraft* was initially only available on home consoles for Microsoft's Xbox 360. Versions for Playstation and Nintendo consoles only followed later.

In earlier versions of *Minecraft*, when there was no World Barrier, completely wild structures were created on the world border. These were called Far Lands by players.

# Short & Sweet

Steps made of wood and stone are probably familiar to every *Minecraft* player. But did you know that Notch once experimented with dirt steps? He used them to test the functionality of the stairs that were later introduced — but the dirt version has not yet made it into the game.

Excluding in-game purchases, approximately 41% of *Minecraft* revenue comes from mobile downloads.

Does Notch ever watch *Minecraft* videos himself? Yes, he admitted when asked about it. But apparently, it feels weird, so he quickly switches to watching non-*Minecraft* videos by Youtubers.

Water owls? Not quite. In the *Bedrock Edition,* the unusual aquatic animals axolotl can turn their heads — in the *Java Edition,* they cannot.

## Special Ears

*Minecraft* creator Notch and music producer Deadmau5 are friends. So, it is no coincidence that Notch has created a unique skin for the Canadian musician — specifically designed as a mouse mask with huge ears, Deadmau5's trademark. The ears cannot be deactivated and are linked to the username "deadmau5".

## A Practical Investment

When Notch announced in September 2014 that he would like to sell his shares in *Minecraft* and Mojang Studios, Phil Spencer, the person responsible at Microsoft, quickly made all the necessary arrangements. Two months later, 2.5 billion dollars were paid — and the pricey deal actually came in quite handy for Microsoft. The US company had already collected this sum in foreign accounts. This meant that the money could not flow into the USA without paying taxes. And so it made more sense to invest the money. In this case, an investment in perhaps the most successful game of all time.

## (Sl)enderman

What does the name "Enderman" remind you of? Slenderman! The creepy internet phenomenon of a tall, slender, faceless man made waves on the internet in the late 2000s. This inspired Notch to invent the Enderman and implement it in *Minecraft.* The monster was supposed to be as scary as possible. This also explains its behavior: Endermen are basically neutral, but if a player makes eye contact with them, they will immediately teleport towards you and chase you — until one of you dies.

## Cancelled Plans

Donating money to support projects — that's how the platform Kickstarter works. In 2014, a particularly dedicated group of *Minecraft* fans got together and announced a project on Kickstarter: If enough money was raised, the group would produce a *Minecraft* fan film. There was only one catch: The group had not obtained any licensing rights from Mojang, so the brand managers had to stop the project. This was probably also because negotiations were already underway for an official *Minecraft* film.

## Inspiration from Afar

A settlement in the End is full of danger, but also full of rare items. These unusually tall and intricate complexes of buildings are located on the islands in the game's End. They are visually reminiscent of Asian pagodas, and this is no coincidence. Before the settlement found its way into *Minecraft,* lead developer Jeb visited the New Summer Palace in China's capital Beijing. He was probably so inspired by the trip that he came up with a design for the settlement.

## Far too Many Zeros

If you were to recreate the surface of our Earth one-to-one in *Minecraft,* you would need more than 510 trillion (written out 510,000,000,000,000) blocks. For the surface of the moon, on the other hand, you would "only" need almost 38 trillion blocks. If you convert this into hard drive space, our planet will require around 464 terabytes (1 TB is 1,000 GB). The moon still makes it to around 35 TB of storage — and we're only talking about a single layer of blocks here.

## A Free House

Between December 2009 and February 2010, you had the opportunity to purchase the so-called *Minecraft Indev Edition.* As the name suggests, this was not a finished edition but an edition in development. In contrast to the *Alpha Edition* of the time, which received regular updates, the *Indev Edition* contained new, partially untested, and highly buggy game elements. This allowed you to participate in the development of *Minecraft* as closely as possible. Also very unusual: Your adventure began in the starting house — an extremely simple wooden block equipped with a few torches. However, this feature was removed in later *Minecraft* editions — as were the new player characters from Dock, which ultimately proved to be too complex (see page 18).

## Males Without a Task

Just like in the real world, turtles in *Minecraft* also return to their birthplace to lay their eggs — but only the females. Turtles were the first animals in the game to have clear gender roles. Only the females produce clusters of eggs, from which between one and four hatchlings will emerge.

## More than Hardcore

The idea for the Hardcore Mode came to Notch when he read a blog entry on a community page. When he later announced the mode in which you lose your score when you die, Notch came up with a joke. He simultaneously announced the "Ultra Hardcore Mode," where you would lose your entire account if you died in the game — luckily, Notch was only joking.

## So Many Cuboids

Pretty complicated: The model of the Ender Dragon consists of 65 blocks, making it the most complex figure in the entire game. Most of the other figures have block numbers in the single digits. When Notch was designing the Ender Dragon, he was afraid he wouldn't be able to create a satisfactory texture because of the number of blocks. That's why he simply programmed software to do this work for him, making it child's play to customize the texture for the Ender Dragon. He even published this program so that the modding community could also play around with the Ender Dragon's appearance.

## Just Like in Real Life

The annual Endercon event takes place during *Minecraft Story Mode.* And there's a little Easter Egg to discover there. In one scene, you can see that Mojang has an exhibition stand in the game as a real developer. You can also see some of the developers and staff there, such as Lydia, who is known as the host of Minecon and also moderates the Endercon in the game, or Jeb, who has been the lead developer of *Minecraft* for many years.

## Fungal Spores in the Fur

Fungi that infest animals like parasites — that's the stuff horror stories are made of. In *Minecraft,* however, this is also the case with the Mooshroom. You can find herds of Mooshrooms in the Mushroom Fields. These cows are normally red in color, and their bodies are covered in mushrooms. When struck by lightning, their color changes to brown. The color can also be reversed in the same way. By the way, if two Mooshrooms of the same color mate, there is a 1 in 1024 chance that a calf of a different color will be born.

Minecraft is only for kids? Think again!

According to Microsoft, the average Minecraft player is 24 years old and male.

## Do-It-Yourself Opponent

A boss monster you can build yourself? That would be the Wither. This three-headed monster comes from the Nether, and you have to build it yourself. To do this, arrange four blocks of Soul Sand or Soul Soil in a T-shape and then place three Wither Skeleton Skulls on top. The monster now comes to life, and you have 11 seconds to seek cover. At the end of this time, the Wither will generate a Strength 7 explosion — the most powerful you can experience in Survival Mode. A chime will sound, heard by all players regardless of dimension, announcing the Wither's awakening. Good luck in battle!

## Small but Mighty

Have you ever experimented with a Raspberry Pi minicomputer? The small and inexpensive devices can be used for a wide variety of projects, from media centers to game servers. An official *Minecraft Pi Edition* was released in 2013. But just three years later, Microsoft discontinued support — meaning that the latest updates are no longer released for the *Pi Edition.*

## Exclusive Club

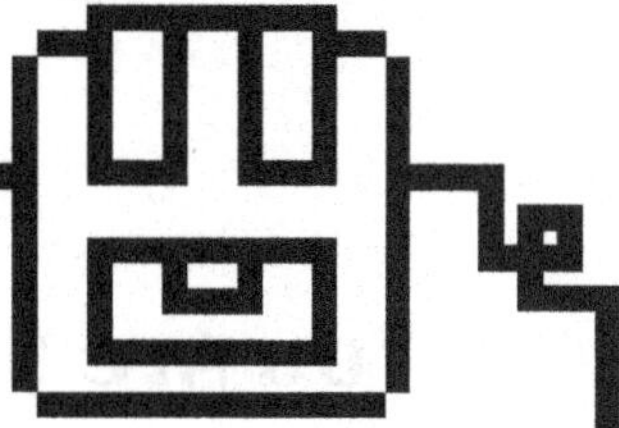

Players in China have also been able to build blocks since 2016 when *Minecraft China* was officially released. Over 600 million downloads were recorded within the first six years. A separate version was created because the Chinese government has strict regulations on game content, which prevents people from around the world from playing the game. You can only log in with a Chinese ID number, so foreigners in China are not allowed to play at all.

## Remotely Saved from the Community

Imagine you are on an exploration tour and want to bring your valuable finds to safety without interrupting your adventure — what do you do then? Quite simple: You use an Ender Chest. The items inside are not stored in the chest itself but in a safe place. This means that your treasures are safe even if the chest is destroyed. The idea for this practical chest came from a player in the community. Seven months later, the Ender Chest was added.

## You Are Not Alone

The character you control in *Minecraft* is not the only one who can collect experience points and level up — at least not entirely. Villagers can reach higher trading levels through bartering. This can be recognized by their badges. With a higher level, they also offer more goods, which vary depending on their profession. The maximum trading level is 250 experience points, which is represented by a level five diamond badge.

## A Hit at Last

The Xbox brand is struggling in Japan. Devices and games from Sony and Nintendo, which are created in the country itself, sell significantly better there. Microsoft, the American company behind Xbox, was therefore probably delighted when *Minecraft* became the first Microsoft game to break the one million physical unit sales mark in Japan at the end of 2019. Although the *Playstation Vita Edition* of *Minecraft* also sold over a million units there, the brand was not yet owned by Microsoft at the time.

## The Pillow Goes Boom

Don't use a bed in the Nether or the End! When Notch added multiple dimensions to *Minecraft*, he faced a problem: Beds are set as Spawn Points when used. However, if you switch dimensions and get killed there, you could be unintentionally teleported to the Nether or the End. To prevent this, Notch came up with a simple trick: If you use a bed in those dimensions, it will simply explode, leaving a crater of destruction in its wake. He called it the simplest solution. Years later, the Respawn Anchor was added, allowing you to set a Spawn Point in the Nether. Beds still explode in the Nether and the End, so be careful there!

## The Thing about Anvils

A truly multifunctional device: You can do a lot with the anvil, such as renaming objects or repairing tools. It's just a shame that the device wears out. On average, you can use an anvil 25 times for your purposes — then it simply disintegrates. An anvil also takes damage when it falls, so it will wear out more quickly.

## Upside Down

Grumm and Dinnerbone are the gamertags of two Mojang developers, Erik Broes and Nathan Adams. Both joined the team in 2012 and have one thing in common — their *Minecraft* avatars are standing upside down. The same thing happens to all other creatures that you call Grumm or Dinnerbone, on their name tags or otherwise.

## The Ancient Scrolls

Mojang probably didn't see this coming: When the Swedish development studio announced its new game called *Scrolls* in March 2011, not everyone in the gaming industry was thrilled — and the first lawsuit was promptly filed. The development studio Bethesda is best known for its game series *The Elder Scrolls,* which includes cult hits such as *Oblivion* and *Skyrim*. Bethesda was concerned that players might confuse the games from Mojang and Bethesda due to the similarity in names. The Swedes subsequently won their case in court and soon after reached an agreement with the American developer. As of now, both Mojang and Bethesda are owned by tech giant Microsoft — which seems slightly ironic in light of the lawsuit.

## Short & Sweet

If you play *Minecraft,* you also watch *Minecraft* videos, right? Not necessarily, because this only applies to a third of boys who play the game. Among girls, the figure is only around nine percent.

In the past, you could often pick up cardboard heads in the Steve design at Mojang and *Minecraft* trade fair stands.

Markus Alexej — these are Notch's two first names. Swap the J for an I, and you have the stage name under which he occasionally releases electronic music.

You block, eat, or aim with the bow and sneak over two layers of Cobweb on a layer of Ice and Soul Sand each — the result is a speed of 0.015 mph or 0.00694445 blocks per second and thus the lowest speed that can be achieved without potions in *Minecraft*.

# Short & Sweet

How often is a new *Minecraft* version tested before release? Very often. Over 20,000 automatic tests were carried out for version 1.18, in addition to the countless test runs by the developers themselves and the game testers.

If you think invisibility hides you from all creatures, you are mistaken. Bats, Villagers, and, of course, cats will always recognize you.

Endermen will attack if you make eye contact — but not if you are wearing a carved pumpkin on your head. Maybe because they can't see where you are looking?

Jack Black meets *Minecraft*? The audiobook of the first *Minecraft* novel was performed by the US actor.

## Just Like the Good Old Days

On April 1, 2019, the time had finally come — the 25-year-old masterpiece *Minecraft 3D* was dug out by Mojang. The classic game won all the awards in 1994, including the Oscar for Best Supporting Actress. Wait a minute, there was no *Minecraft* or Mojang in the 1990s. Was there? That's right, the pranksters had pulled another one of their infamous April Fools' pranks and released a video of *Minecraft* as it would have looked in the 1990s. Apart from a few more pixels, there weren't too many differences to be seen. This version was even playable for users of the *Minecraft Java Edition*.

## Vicious Villager

Those evil Illagers! Evokers, Pillagers, Vindicators — none of them are exactly friendly to you and the Villagers. But where does this strange name come from? When Mojang wanted to add another enemy to the Zombies, Skeletons, and the like, there was always talk of the evil — ill-minded — Villager. Put the words together and you get the portmanteau "Illager".

## A Children's Game in an Adult Series

The adult-oriented animation series *South Park* is known for making fun of pop culture phenomena. So, it was only a matter of time before the show's creators, Matt Stone and Trey Parker, started making fun of *Minecraft.* In the fall of 2013, the time had finally come. According to Stone and Parker, *Minecraft* is the first video game whose appeal Stone and Parker cannot understand, making it the perfect "victim".

But before the *South Park* producers ventured into this parody, they warned Notch and Mojang and asked for their permission. The response? Mojang sent the *South Park* team a merchandise package, and Notch told them they could incorporate *Minecraft* into the series however they liked. The episode went down extremely well with the *Minecraft* creator. He ate a whole bag of popcorn while watching it, as he revealed online.

## Few Inhabitants, but Many Viewers

With over 111 million subscribers, Swede Pewdiepie is one of the most successful Youtubers of all time. His Let's Play videos for horror games such as *Amnesia — The Dark Descent* have brought him his international breakthrough, partly because he has commented on them in English. However, his very first video looked completely different: *Minecraft Multiplayer Fun* was uploaded in October 2010 and is just under two minutes long. In it, Pewdiepie still speaks in Swedish and does not show his face. Despite this, the video has been clicked on around 22 million times so far — with a population of almost 11 million, it's as if everyone in Sweden has watched it twice.

## Beard Again After 13 Years

Not a warm smile? Originally, Steve was bearded, which was often mistaken for a smile. With the Survival Test Update 0.24, Steve was given a shave. Almost 13 years later, the beard is back in the game, thanks to an update. Interestingly, most of the promotional graphics for the game during this time still featured a bearded Steve.

## Surviving Differently

Before Notch started working on *Minecraft*, his focus was on a game called *Zombie Town*. He cited games such as *Left 4 Dead* and *GTA — Chinatown Wars* as sources of inspiration. When Notch finally started programming *Minecraft* in May 2009, he needed a player character. He simply adopted the character from *Zombie Town,* as its design was a perfect fit for the new, blocky cave adventure. So, the character we know today as Steve was actually a survivor from Notch's unreleased game *Zombie Town.*

## Great Rewards

Isn't it nice to be rewarded for accomplishing something? In the *Minecraft Bedrock Edition,* this is exactly what Achievements are for. You can collect 125 of them by completing certain tasks, and some of them unlock items and emotes for your character. In the *Java Edition,* your Achievements are measured by progress — they work exactly the same way.

## Traps and Moss

You come across a Jungle Temple or Jungle Pyramid and want to get to the valuable Chests but don't feel like disarming the dangerous traps or solving the puzzle? Simply use a pickaxe to get through. This method may take a little longer, but it will get you there. And maybe you could use some Mossy Cobblestone, anyway.

## Survival Games

If you played *Minecraft* on a console before the stand-alone console version was replaced by the *Bedrock Edition,* then you may have seen the Mini-games option in the main menu. This gives you access to three different Multiplayer Modes. You can compete with other players in battle arenas — either in direct duels or in Tumble Mode, where you literally have to pull the ground out from under your opponents' feet. And if you're more in the mood for an obstacle course, then Glide Mode is just the thing for you. These modes are only available on old console versions.

## Dangerous Toast

If you name a rabbit "Toast", it will change its appearance to a special one — white with a black rump and ears. The same applies to the now-deleted Killer Bunnies, which have white fur and red eyes. Although they look as harmless as any other rabbit, they will continue to attack you relentlessly. By the way: This feature is in memory of the missing rabbit "Toast", which belonged to the girlfriend of the player "xyzen420".

## Guitar Craft Saga

From guitars to blocks to sweets: US developer Ryan Holtz started his career working on games such as *Guitar Hero* before joining Mojang in November 2013. Among other things, he was responsible for customizing *Minecraft's* game world and implementing rabbits. Less than two years later, in April 2015, he moved on to King, the development studio behind *Candy Crush*. His announcement on April 1 was initially thought to be a joke, but the following day, he confirmed once again that he was indeed no longer working on *Minecraft*.

As you can imagine, developing a game is not easy. That's why Notch officially founded the Mojang studio in 2009 and hired people to help him.

The name comes from the Swedish word for device – mojäng.

## Playing in the Freezing Cold

Only a few thousand people live in Antarctica. With such extreme temperatures outside, what do the researchers do in their spare time? That's right, they play *Minecraft* — or at least some of them do, according to Mojang. Consequently, *Minecraft* has already been played on all seven continents of the world.

### Do Whatever You Want

*Minecraft* in another game? *The Stanley Parable* makes it possible. In the PC and console game, a narrator guides you through the world. Depending on which path you choose and whether or not you listen to the narrator's words, different game endings are possible. In one ending, the narrator even takes you into a typical *Minecraft* world, has a hut built in front of you, and gives you commands to collect resources. In the end, he gives *Minecraft* a score of one out of five.

## Bon Appetit

Would you try a Golden Apple in real life — or maybe even Spider Eyes? Youtuber Preston did just that. In a self-experiment, he ate only things that can be found in *Minecraft* for 24 hours. And in another video, he hired a chef to cook *Minecraft* dishes for him. He then ranked them. Unsurprisingly, Preston put both Golden Apple and Cake in first place.

## Many Bright Colors

Rainbow Crystal Caves in *Minecraft*? This colorful idea was suggested as new game content by a fan in the old feedback forum in February 2011 — and marked as planned by Mojang. But after numerous years of waiting, nothing has happened in this direction, and the old feedback forum has also been shut down. So, it is more than doubtful that you will ever be able to explore Rainbow Crystal Caves.

## Misfortune

13 hearts: This is what the health points of the Witches look like in *Minecraft.* Quite strange, as many mobs tend to have 10 hearts. This is probably due to the common superstition that 13 is an unlucky number and is often associated with the occult. Since Witches can probably be counted as occult beings, this number of hearts fits perfectly.

## Less Talking, More Crafting

How can the mechanics of trading be transferred into a game in a sensible way? This was the problem the developers at Mojang faced when introducing Villagers to *Minecraft.* Many role-playing games have text-heavy trading menus, but this would not fit in with the relatively text-poor rest of *Minecraft*. The developers experimented with the idea of having speech bubbles pop up above the Villagers to represent their trade offers. However, this system would have been limited and confusing, so the decision was made not to use speech bubbles. Now, you can simply see what is on offer and at what price in a text-free trading window. That's handy!

## Short & Sweet

Redstone cables cannot transmit a signal indefinitely. On a flat surface, the signal will travel a maximum of 15 blocks. After that, the signal disappears — unless a Redstone Repeater is installed.

Although the scary character Herobrine does not appear in any of the *Minecraft* games, he does make appearances in various official promotional graphics, such as in some Lego instructions.

Jeb's cat also served as inspiration: When the developer wanted to incorporate cats into the game, his beloved "Newton" had to be the model.

The Guinness Book of Records lists over 200 *Minecraft*-related records — from the longest Redstone track to the largest replica of a national flag, pretty much everything is represented.

# Short & Sweet

Smithing Templates allow you to change the appearance of your armor. The Silence Template is the rarest: It can only be found in Chests in the already rare Ancient City in the Deep Dark. However, it has a low drop rate of only 1.2%.

Some of the painting graphics in *Minecraft* feature elements from other video games. These include, for example, the scaffolding from *Donkey Kong*, parts of the "de_aztec" map from *Counter Strike*, and the fighters from *International Karate Plus.*

If you kill a Slime, it may split into smaller Slimes, and you will have to fight several enemies at the same time. If the Slime has been given a name by a name tag, for example, this name will be passed on to all the smaller versions.

## Level Up

You've probably seen them before — those little green balls that ring when you pick them up. They contain experience points that you can use to increase your level. This has no direct effect on your character. Instead, you can invest your collected experience in things like armor repair or enchantments. Experience orbs are dropped by various actions, and you lose them again when you die. The bigger and more yellow the orbs are, the more experience they give you. For example, the Ender Dragon drops one with a red dot in the middle.

## Not so Fast

Every panda has a mind of its own. Lazy pandas are known to be among the slowest land creatures in *Minecraft.* Only newly hatched turtles move even more sluggishly on their way to the water. Once submerged, however, they pick up speed and can even overtake Drowned. The fact that lazy pandas are so extremely slow, makes them a particularly exotic pet — but leading them home can be an everlasting task.

## A Vision of Our Own

When asked about the modding community, Notch admitted that he initially felt threatened. The reason: It felt like someone was reinterpreting his vision of *Minecraft.* But Notch quickly understood how important mods were for the game and how much they had contributed to the success of *Minecraft.* That's why he has never regretted simply letting the modding community run wild. Looking back, it was the right thing to do, as some modifications have even gone on to become official game content. And the *Minecraft* marketplace would certainly not exist without the many ideas from the community that have influenced *Minecraft* over the years.

## On a Secret Quest

Can you solve the puzzle? Mojang developer Michael Stoyke, also known as Searge, has built a reputation for adding secret features to *Minecraft* that have never been publicly announced. Resourceful *Minecraft* fans set out in search of these secret functions and shared their findings online.

## Eight Years without a Face

*Minecraft* Youtuber Dream hid behind a mask for a long time. It looks like a simple, white, grinning smiley face and has become his trademark over the years. There was just one problem: It made some video ideas impossible to realize. Clay, Dream's real name, no longer wanted to be restricted and dropped the mask. However, the reactions to the unveiling of his face were unusually controversial. Some fans were surprised that Dream didn't look "dreamy", as his name suggests, but simply normal. A wave of memes and jokes swept through his fanbase, and Dream's unveiling video was viewed almost 22 million times on the first day — it has now been clicked more than 60 million times.

Eight months later, Dream released a follow-up video. In it, he explained that he regretted his revelation as it had brought him too much attention and hatred. As a result, he was going to wear a smiley mask again in the future and delete all images and videos of his face from the internet. Dream wanted to focus on his *Minecraft* videos undisturbed. A few months later, however, he at least posted his unveiling video again. A nice message because hate has no place on the internet and in *Minecraft*.

## Formerly Known As ...

*Minecraft* is simply called *Minecraft*. However, early prototype versions of the game still bore the subtitle *Order of the Stone* before Notch simply dropped it. The title was picked up again in *Minecraft Story Mode.* There, the legendary hero group is called "The Order of the Stone".

## Something Like Burn-out?

A key reason why Notch publicly offered to sell the *Minecraft* brand in 2014 was the extreme pressure he was under. Working on *Minecraft* and at developer studio Mojang was said to be exhausting, as was the enormous media attention. Notch was also unable to cope with the public pressure. After all, millions of players always have expectations that are almost impossible to fulfill and that Notch no longer wanted to meet.

## Don't Look at the Scale

A strict diet? In early concepts, the pandas were much slimmer. However, Mojang quickly realized that a stockier figure was much better suited to the lovable bears. That's why the pandas were fed plenty of pixelated bamboo before they grew to their current size — at least, that's how the people in charge at Mojang put it.

## What a Drama

It is only a matter of time before the most successful video game of all time is made into a movie. Mojang was approached by Hollywood producers back in 2012 but quickly turned them down. At the time, it was said that a movie adaptation of *Minecraft* would only be seriously considered if someone came to Mojang with the right idea. Two years later, it was announced that an agreement had been reached with Warner Bros. Pictures. In the years that followed, however, there was a lot of back and forth. Numerous changes in directors and screenwriters meant that production was restarted several times and the *Minecraft* movie was delayed again and again.

## Committed Developers and Players

Jeb published his own online multiplayer role-playing game, *Whispers in Akarra,* in 2001 at the age of just 22. Although he had to abandon the project in February 2004, he still managed to entertain hundreds of players with his work in just under three years. Somewhat later, Jeb even released the game's source code, allowing dedicated modders in the fan community to keep *Whispers in Akarra* alive on private servers.

### Self-Made Notch

How did Notch learn to program? According to his own statement, he taught himself. When he was seven years old, his father bought a Commodore computer, and just a few years later, little Notch was developing his first text-based adventure game on it. His knowledge of game design, i.e., how games work and are structured, came from playing a lot over the years. He was, therefore, able to successfully apply this knowledge to the development of *Minecraft.*

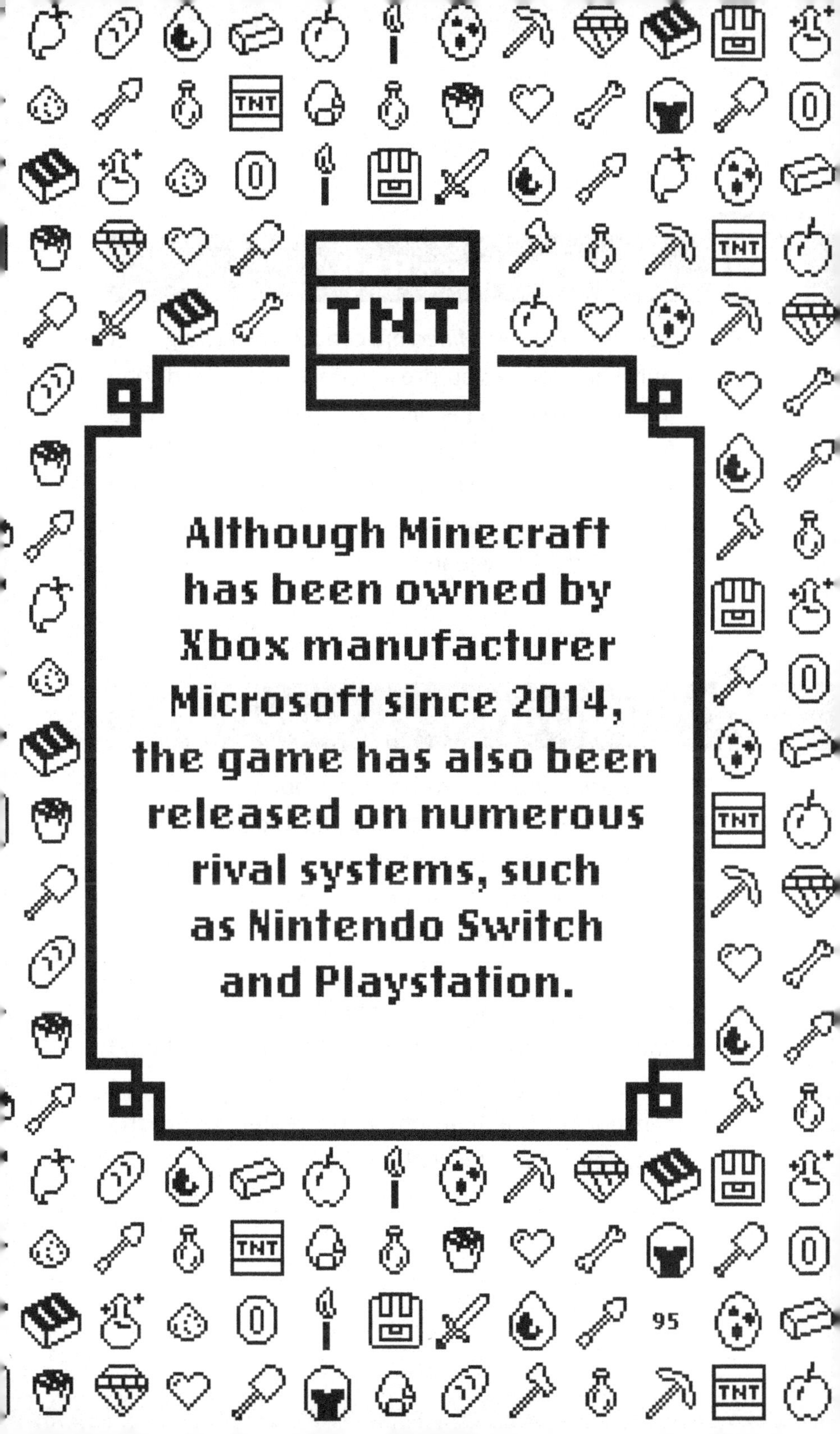

Although Minecraft has been owned by Xbox manufacturer Microsoft since 2014, the game has also been released on numerous rival systems, such as Nintendo Switch and Playstation.

## Anti-Creeper Ball

Keeping a cat in *Minecraft* can be rewarding. Not only will it bring you presents every now and then in the morning — just like cats in real life. Having a four-legged furball around in the game also keeps Creepers and Phantoms away. The latter are hissed at as a warning, but they never actually attack. Talk about fluffy bodyguards!

## Minecraft Meets Lovecraft

They are supposed to be scary, but scary in a different way: Wardens and Sculk Blocks look like they come from another world. This is because the Mojang developers wanted to create a mysterious creepiness, so they looked to the horror worlds of author H. P. Lovecraft for inspiration. It is less about shocking horror and more about the fear of the unknown and the incomprehensible. Mojang should be satisfied with the result. After all, 175 different concepts for the Wardens were created before the final design was decided on.

# Short & Sweet

Diamonds are extremely rare in *Minecraft* — and non-renewable. Nevertheless, it is possible to purchase diamond products, such as armor and tools, through bartering.

Silverfish can infest certain stone blocks. If you mine such a block, the little insects will spawn.

Would you have known that? Around 80% of all *Minecraft* players are male — only around 20% are female.

*Minecraft Education* provides deep insights into the blocky game world. You can learn that Redstone Dust is made up of 31% uranium and 31% carbon. The remaining 38% is made up of an undiscovered substance. This means that Redstone Dust is radioactive due to its uranium content.

# Short & Sweet

If you dismantle a decorative Head Block, it will disintegrate from the outside to the inside. The opposite is true for all other blocks — they disintegrate from the inside out.

Since 2017, novels set in the *Minecraft* universe have been published on a regular basis. More than 15 official novels have now been published, selling over five million copies in total.

Are souls trapped in the Soul Sand? Judging by its texture, yes. After all, there are three screaming faces on it. Will they be freed one day?

Notch had once planned to allow you to use your own motifs for paintings. However, this feature never made it into the game.

## Exploring, Dreaming, and Discovering

When you play through *Minecraft,* an inspirational quote appears after the end dialog and credits. It says that you should live your life so you have no regrets in the future. In early versions of the game, the quote was mistakenly attributed to American author Mark Twain. However, after it was pointed out to Notch that this was not one of his quotes, Twain's name was replaced with "Unknown" — although many people still assume that Twain is the author.

## Simply Rub with Honey

Just like in the real world, copper can also turn green in *Minecraft.* This process is called oxidation. However, if you want to prevent this, there is a simple trick. You can wax your copper blocks with Honeycomb. This will ensure that they maintain their state, i.e., they either stop oxidizing or retain their oxidation level.

## The Food of My Food

Is this cannibalism? The two-legged pig monsters Piglins feed mainly on Hoglins, the wild boar-like monsters that also live in the Nether. You can also use them as a source of food. Although hostile to you, Hoglins can be bred. The only other hostile monsters that can still be bred are the Killer Bunnies, which have been removed from the official game content — but you can still spawn them by command.

## Undead Sailors

Drowned can simply spawn in the water — or they can be created when Zombies remain underwater for more than 30 seconds. They will then undergo an irreversible transformation that lasts a few seconds. It is also possible for Drowned Chicken Jockeys to spawn in the sea in *Minecraft Java Edition.* The chicken will then drive them to the surface. During the day, however, the sunlight burns the undead Drowned. So, if you ever discover a chicken in rough seas, it will have previously been the mount of a Drowned.

## Pixels You Can Touch

Nintendo and Microsoft are actually competitors, as both companies sell their own consoles on the video game market. However, their relationship is often characterized by a lack of animosity. Microsoft games appear on Nintendo consoles time and again — such as *Ori and the Blind Forest* or, of course, *Minecraft*.

To celebrate *Minecraft's* release for the Nintendo 3DS family in Europe, the two companies collaborated once again. In October 2018, a limited-edition New Nintendo 2DS XL version was released in the Creeper design — typically green with a pixelated grim face and blocky relief on the front, the handheld looks explosively fun.

The design was created by Lydia Winters, who you may know as the presenter of the Minecon livestreams. Her original idea was a Grass Block design, but an Xbox One console had already been released in this style, which is why the nasty Creeper face was ultimately chosen.

## A Fair Choice

To celebrate the release of *Minecraft* in China, Mojang held a survey for fans in the Far East in September 2018. They were able to choose which national treasure should find its way into the game: the panda, the Thorold's deer, the Chinese alligator, the golden snub-nosed monkey, or the Chinese river dolphin. Naturally, the panda won the vote and was added to *Minecraft* about six months later. If you ever want to meet a panda, all you have to do is look for them in the Jungle biomes.

## It's All in the Mix

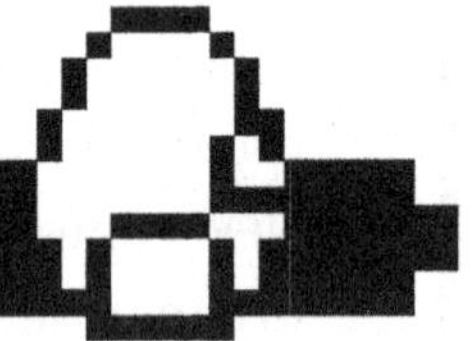

When *Minecraft* meets another popular universe, this result is called a "mash-up". Basic elements such as gameplay, music, or textures can be completely replaced. You can purchase these add-ons directly from the in-game store — at least in the *Minecraft Bedrock Edition.* Well-known mash-ups include the *Halo* package or the *Super Mario* mash-up, which is exclusive to Nintendo consoles but free of charge.

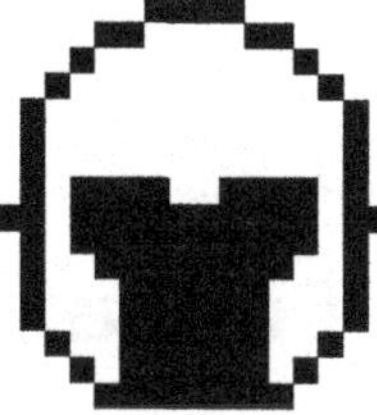

## Here and There

Can you guess which countries *Minecraft* is most popular in? Around 21% of active *Minecraft* players live in the USA, making it by far the largest community. This is followed by Brazil with around 6.2% and Russia with just under 6%. Players from the UK make up about 5%.

## A Different Sort of Evil

As you know, creatures in *Minecraft* are not normally assigned to a gender. However, Notch once announced that the Ender Dragon was a female creature called "Jean". Mojang developer Nathan "Dinnerbone" Adams also repeated this name, describing the final boss as female. In fact, the Ender Dragon is the only creature you can't assign a name tag because, according to the official *Minecraft* website, revealing its true name would unleash a destructive force. Yet, "Jean" sounds pretty peaceful ...

## Enchanting

Beware the Dark Forest! Dark Oak Trees and Huge Mushrooms grow in this biome, and the trees are so crowded together that the sun hardly gets through the canopy, allowing monsters to spawn even during the day. Witches also hide in their forest estates in this biome. For this reason, many players refer to the Dark Forest as the Enchanted Forest.

### The Hidden Creeper

Are you exploring a cave and suddenly hear eerie noises? These ambient sounds can send shivers down your spine. The so-called *Cave 14* sound is particularly notorious — not just because it conveys a creepy atmosphere, but because there is more to it than that. If you examine the soundtrack in a spectrogram — a program that displays sounds visually — the face of a Creeper becomes clearly recognizable. Creepy!

## Small but Blubblub

Fox cubs in *Minecraft* are not only incredibly cute — they are also tiny. So tiny, in fact, that when they swim, they can't get their heads above the water's surface and end up drowning. This is particularly evident when the cubs are hunting for fish. Fortunately, you can rescue them, as unlike adult animals, fox cubs trust the player.

## No Time for Seasons

Back in 2013, it became public that Mojang was experimenting with different seasons in *Minecraft.* For example, trees would change color in fall, and the days would be shorter than in summer. However, more than 10 years later, such a seasonal feature has still not made it into the game, so it is highly questionable whether it will ever be implemented. If you still want to enjoy seasons in *Minecraft,* you will have to resort to fan modifications, for better or worse.

## From Blocky to Pointed

In real life, you can find stalactites and stalagmites in caves. In *Minecraft,* you can also find their counterparts, called Pointed Dripstones. However, when the Mojang developers were planning this unusual block for the game, they faced a problem: Such pointed shapes look out of place in a game dominated by square blocks and stand out too much in *Minecraft's* environment. That's why the art designers came up with the idea of modeling the pointed stalactites after plants that had already been added, coloring them in a stony, earthy color. This gives the Dripstone a completely natural look.

## Quite Annoying

Bats fly around wildly and can get on your nerves with their beeping. Yet, their agility makes them particularly difficult to kill. If you do manage to kill one, you can expect — nothing. Bats drop neither items nor experience points. Their uselessness, makes some players wonder why they were added to *Minecraft* in the first place. Maybe there isn't a point to everything?

# Short & Sweet

If you play *Minecraft* on a PC and open the inventory, you may notice the direction your character is looking. It is always looking towards the mouse pointer as if it were watching it.

If you type "excitedze" — the in-game name of Mojang developer Maria Lemón — into the recipe book, your in-game language will change to pirate. This is a reference to the programmer of the recipe book, whose *Minecraft* avatar is dressed like a pirate.

Skeletons and Zombies can pick up decorative Head Blocks and wear them like helmets — so a Skeleton can also put on a Skeleton Skull.

Around 54% of boys aged 12 and younger have played *Minecraft* at least once. This figure is slightly lower for girls at around 46%.

# Short & Sweet

Trick or treat! At Halloween time, monsters such as Skeletons and Zombies wear pumpkins on their heads.

Getting lost in a blocky corn maze — that sounds like fun. Back in 2015, Jeb once said that he could imagine Corn Blocks in *Minecraft*. Unfortunately, this idea has not yet come to fruition.

Mojang put together a team with hardly any experience in creating mobs. The result was the Sniffer, an ancient creature that only hatches from eggs found in Ocean Ruins.

If your cat is sitting on a Chest, you'll have to be patient because you can't open it like that. Typical cat behavior.

## In a Land Before Time

That old already?! Freedonia is the official world record holder for the oldest *Minecraft* server. Less than an hour after Notch activated the multiplayer function for the Survival Mode on August 4, 2010, the Freedonia server was launched — and has not been shut down since. The world has grown to over 40 kilometers in diameter, and more than 270,000 players have already entered the blocks of Freedonia.

## The Slightly Different Way to Gamble

Want to play *Minecraft* instead of streaming series or movies? You can with the Amazon Fire TV Stick and Apple TV streaming devices — at least to some extent. This is because there have been no new up-dates since 2021. However, if you are happy with an outdated version of *Minecraft,* you can still have fun on streaming devices.

## Tit for Tat

*Minecraft* has inspired many other video games, such as the 2D crafting game *Terraria*. However, *Terraria* has also had a certain influence on *Minecraft*. Lead developer Jeb has admitted that he was inspired by *Terraria's* boss spawn mechanic, where a boss monster is summoned by the player. More specifically, it inspired the idea of the Wither. That kind of spawn is exactly what Jeb was looking for. The occult theme that comes with it fits perfectly with the undead Wither.

## Hiding Places in the Snow

You can come across igloos in snow-covered areas, and every other igloo has an underground laboratory. Its entrance is covered by a carpet. A Villager and a Zombie are trapped inside. If you use the materials in the laboratory to heal the Zombie, you can build a new village with the two rescued Villagers.

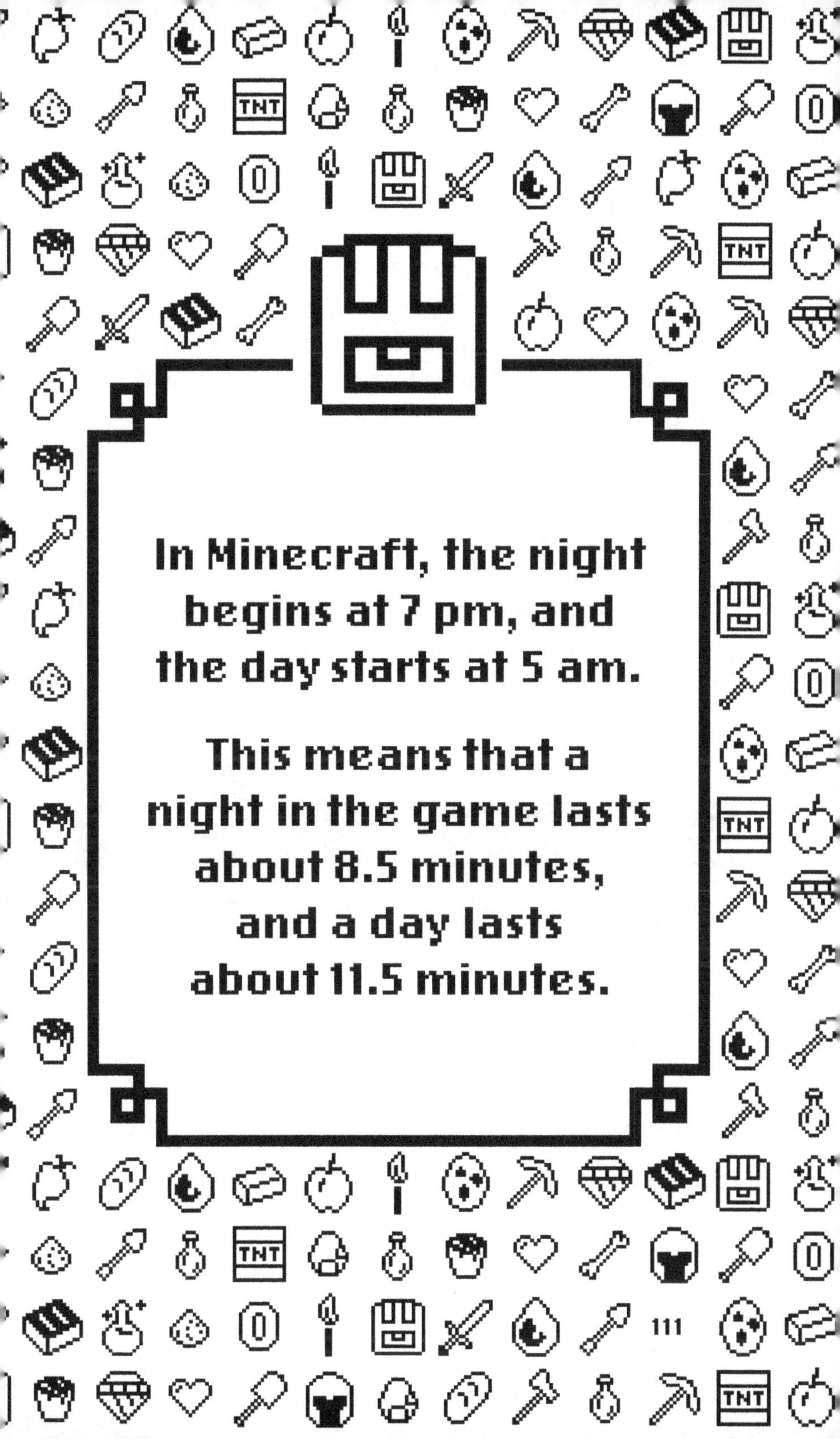

In Minecraft, the night begins at 7 pm, and the day starts at 5 am.

This means that a night in the game lasts about 8.5 minutes, and a day lasts about 11.5 minutes.

## Bonus Round

After Steve and Alex had found their way into the fighting game *Super Smash Bros. Ultimate* as fighters in October 2020, their matching Amiibo figures — small figures that can be used to unlock content on Nintendo consoles — were released almost two years later in September 2022. These are also compatible with other games. For example, if you scan the Steve Amiibo while playing *Kirby and the Forgotten Land*, you will receive extra coins and items. Ironically, the Steve and Alex Amiibo figures are not compatible with the Nintendo versions of *Minecraft*.

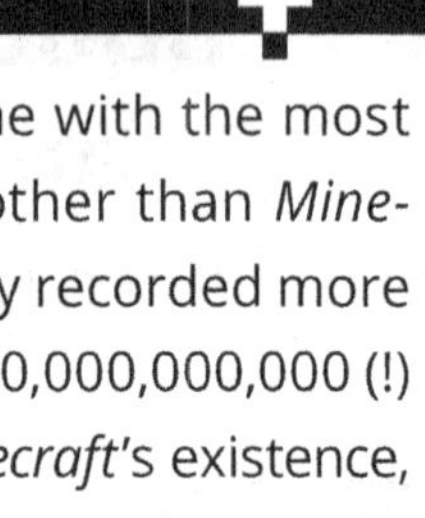

## One with 12 Zeros

Not *Fortnite*, nor *Roblox* — the game with the most video views on Youtube is none other than *Minecraft*. Our favorite game has already recorded more than one trillion views — that's 1,000,000,000,000 (!) views. In the first eight years of *Minecraft*'s existence, there were "only" 500 billion views. It took just two more years to reach the next 500 billion. This shows that *Minecraft* is more popular than ever.

## Simpcraft

Steve in yellow? *Minecraft* has found its way into modern pop culture. So, it's not surprising that the iconic *Simpsons* have also made references to the blocky world. In April 2014, when the entire intro to an episode was drawn in *Minecraft* style — including an exploding Creeper at the end — Notch in particular couldn't believe it. According to him, it still felt like he was developing a little game in his home.

## Meowing at the Full Moon

Do black cats bring bad luck? That's just superstition. So, if you are interested in a furry companion, there are various ways to get your hands on a black cat. Firstly, you can visit one of the rare Swamp Huts, where the four-legged friends are guaranteed to spawn — but watch out for the evil Witches! You can also keep your eyes open on the night of a full moon. The chance of seeing a black cat increases to 50%, then.

## Humpbacked Bears?

Adding new creatures to *Minecraft* isn't always a smooth process. First, concept drawings are made, and initial models are created to test the behavior of the new mobs in-game. After all, Mojang considers *Minecraft* one large ecosystem. If it is deemed suitable, the actual implementation can begin. But even that doesn't always work the first time. The first camel models, for example, still looked more like teddy bears with humps. It was only after a few adjustments that they were successfully transformed into a camel, creating a mob that, according to Mojang, immediately won over all the developers.

## No Discounts

There are a number of tricks you can use in the trading window. For example, it is easier to kill or kidnap the Villagers in question while trading. And if your trading partner dies in the meantime, the menu will stay open for a while, and you can still make deals. A strange thought.

## Panic Underground

Do you dare to play the Hardcore Mode? The difficulty isn't just set to hard — if you die in the game, you will stay dead, and your saved game will be unusable. Twitch streamer Philza had to learn this the hard way; during a hardcore run that lasted over five years, he was surprised by a Baby Zombie in enchanted golden armor. His attacks had little effect, and he himself took permanent damage. In a panic, he tried to run away and was killed by a spider — and lost his score of the last five years. To this day, Philza holds the record for the longest sustained run in Hardcore Mode.

## Well-Hidden ... But Why?

What's that doing there? In the game files for the game *Fire Pro Wrestling World* by Japanese developers Zex Corporation and Spike Chunsuft, the latter of whom was responsible for the *Pokémon Mystery Dungeon* series, there are texture skins of the pig from *Minecraft*. However, these do not appear in the wrestling game itself and are not used. Pretty funny!

## Fan-Made

Mojang handles the *Minecraft* trademark license very carefully. All license applications are processed directly by Mojang and reviewed by the artistic and marketing management. Cheap, mass-produced items are not licensed, nor are typical decorative items. Mojang sees *Minecraft* much more as a creative playground and encourages fans to express their creativity in the real world by creating their own *Minecraft* decorative items.

## No Rose for You

In early versions of *Minecraft*, you could still find roses everywhere in the game world. However, as more and more types of flowers were added over time, the developers at Mojang came up with an idea. With the introduction of rose bushes, which grow more realistically than individual roses anyway, they became more or less redundant. So, it was decided to replace roses with poppies. There are now around 15 different types of flowers in *Minecraft*.

## Substance from Distant Biomes

The Swamp biome is dotted with oaks; you won't find any other kind of tree here. Nevertheless, the Swamp Huts of the Witches who live there are made from a different type of wood: spruce. Spruce tends to be found in cold biomes such as the Taiga or the Mountains. So, the question arises: How do Witches actually get a hold of the distant Spruces?

## Everyone Starts Small

0

*Minecraft* celebrated its first Christmas in the winter of 2009, and Notch came up with a very special promotion. You could give the game away completely for free for three weeks. In total, 1,436 people were able to enjoy a free version of *Minecraft.* By comparison, the game only sold 361 times on a regular basis during the same period. But Notch wasn't complaining. On the contrary, he was happy about every new player. During these three weeks, he also accepted donations to support the development of *Minecraft,* which was still in its beginnings at the time. The result was the incredible sum of about 74 dollars. Still better than nothing!

## Seven Times Our Earth

There are around 60 million blocks from one end of the *Minecraft* world to the other, which is about 37,000 miles in the real world. To put this in perspective, the circumference of the Earth is around 25,000 miles. Since a square area is more spacious than a spread-out sphere, the maximum *Minecraft* world of about 1.4 billion square miles is seven times larger than the area of our Earth, which is about 200 million square miles.

## Ice Without Penguins

Many players reacted with joy to the announcement that icebergs and dolphins would be added to *Minecraft.* However, as is so often the case, it was not possible to make everyone happy. One fan asked about penguins, and Jeb's answer was simple: "Not this time." However, when asked whether this meant that penguins would still be added to *Minecraft* in future updates, Jeb didn't get back to us. And to this day, the popular birds are not in *Minecraft*.

## Bears at Last

Jeb's wife is a huge bear fan — so much so that there is a room in their home completely furnished with bear paraphernalia. For years, his wife had been begging *Minecraft's* lead programmer to finally add a bear to the game. Jeb's answer? If they had a bear of their own, the furry animals would find their way into *Minecraft*. And he was true to his word. When his son was born, the couple named him "Björn" — which translates to "bear" in Swedish. Jeb then added polar bears to *Minecraft*.

## How Lucky Are You?

Chickens are probably the only creatures in *Minecraft* that don't need a partner to reproduce, as they lay eggs all by themselves. When you open them, there is a 12.5% chance that a chick will hatch — and the probability of four of them hatching at the same time is around 0.39%. If you are particularly lucky and you manage to do this with each batch of 16 eggs, you could theoretically "hatch" up to 64 chicks.

## Learning by Playing

*Minecraft* as a school subject? What sounds too good to be true is a reality in Sweden. In 2013, Viktor Rydberg Middle School introduced a new compulsory subject. The aim is to teach students the basics of urban planning, environmental contexts, and setting goals for the future. Teachers are enthusiastic about it and rate the project as a success.

## Red Dust in the PC

Microsoft is known for including references to its games in its Windows operating system. A good example of this is the Cortana voice assistant: In the *Halo* series, Cortana is the artificial assistant helping the protagonist Master Chief. It is therefore not surprising that *Minecraft* references have also found their way into the Windows operating system. Between 2016 and 2018, no less than five updates were named "Redstone" — just like the conductive dust that you can use to interactively design various construction projects in *Minecraft.*

## Short & Sweet

Have you spotted Steve in games other than *Minecraft*? The brand's figurehead has made one or two guest appearances over the years. For example, he is a playable character in *Retro City Rampage,* and there is a Steve head item in *Borderlands 2.*

If you fall through a Cobweb, your speed is only about seven centimeters (about 2.8 inches) per second. Therefore, a drop takes around 26 seconds to fall through a Cobweb.

If you are interested in *Minecraft* Lego, there are over 120 different sets to choose from.

In the trailer for Mojang's card game *Scrolls,* Jeb, the lead programmer behind *Minecraft,* was referred to as *gingerwithasoul* (redhead-with-a-soul). This is an allusion to the common internet joke that redheads do not have a soul.

# Short & Sweet

In Notch's side project *Minicraft*, which was released in December 2011, there were already item storing objects that functioned similarly to Shulker Boxes — almost five years before they were introduced in *Minecraft*.

If you communicate with your friends via iMessenger, you also have an official *Minecraft* sticker pack at your disposal — at least if you purchase it for just about two dollars.

It was only after the Far Lands were removed from the game via an update that one of the splash texts on the start screen read "Check out the Far Lands!"

The intensity of the green of the Grass Blocks varies depending on the biome. The Grass Block found in the Jungle is the brightest green.

## Steve Himself

Got a great idea that you think should be in the game? Then, be sure to check out the official *Minecraft* feedback website. As well as reporting bugs or asking questions about the game, you can also share your own suggestions and ideas — and who knows, the next block might be based on your invention.

## It's Better If You Walk

They are among the strongest creatures in *Minecraft,* and not even the boss monsters can keep up with them: the Wardens. They may be blind, but their senses of hearing and smell work just fine. Once they come after you, the only way to escape is to run — or at least, that was the developers' intention. For this reason, the Wardens originally did not drop anything, so that the player would not even be tempted to try and eliminate these terrible creatures. However, as is so often the case, the player community has different ideas than the developers and sees Wardens as a challenge simply because of their enormous level of difficulty. In the end, Mojang gave them an item to drop: the Sculk Catalyst. This is a block that generates decorative sculk when creatures die in its vicinity.

## Like in a Sandbox

Build and play as you please — games that offer such an open principle are called sandbox games. And *Minecraft* is probably the best-known representative of this type. Some inventors take the sandbox principle to such an extreme that they introduce new ways of playing. The term actually comes from the metaphor of a sandbox game, where a separate world is created with its own rules. The term was used for video games as early as the 1980s.

## A Wet Mishap

*Minecraft Classic Edition* uses outdated game physics. This means that you can flood the entire world with a single bucket of liquid — water or lava. Liquids were not limited back then, which is why they spread infinitely. Fortunately, this is no longer possible in modern versions of *Minecraft.* Notch himself has admitted that he once accidentally flooded a server he was only a guest on with a bucket of water. Oops!

## Everything Leads to the Cow

Have you ever heard of the Moobloom? It's a cow overgrown with buttercups. Unfortunately, this unusual animal only appeared in the now-defunct *Minecraft Earth* app. There, the yellow cow left a trail of dandelions and the occasional sunflower. In the mob vote for the Minecraft Live 2020 event, you could vote to add the Moobloom to the main game. However, the vote was unfavorable for the yellow cow. It came last in the vote. Instead, glow-in-the-dark fish were integrated into *Minecraft.* At the moment, it doesn't look like we'll be seeing the flowery cow again in the future. What a pity!

## The World Is Not Black and White

Look at the world from a completely different perspective. If you click on a Creeper in Spectator Mode, the game world appears green and slightly pixelated. Click on an Enderman, and the colors are reversed to negative. And if you look at the world from a spider's perspective, your field of vision is quintupled.

## Of Pandas and Bees

Play *Minecraft* and save the world? A collaboration with WWF (World Wide Fund For Nature) makes it possible. The collaboration has been in place since 2018 and initially focused on raising awareness of the panda population. After players planted a total of 10 million blocks of Bamboo to create in-game panda reserves, Mojang donated 100,000 dollars to the WWF. The merchandise proceeds from the corresponding collections were also donated to a good cause. In the years that followed, attention was drawn to the importance of bees.

## Soft and Hard

Just like in the real world, Concrete Powder in *Minecraft* is not a solid mass. Instead, the material behaves like sand or gravel — Concrete Powder Blocks are affected by gravity. However, when such a block comes into contact with water, it immediately hardens and turns into a Concrete Block. These blocks are then solid and do not care about gravity. Rain has no effect whatsoever on Concrete Powder.

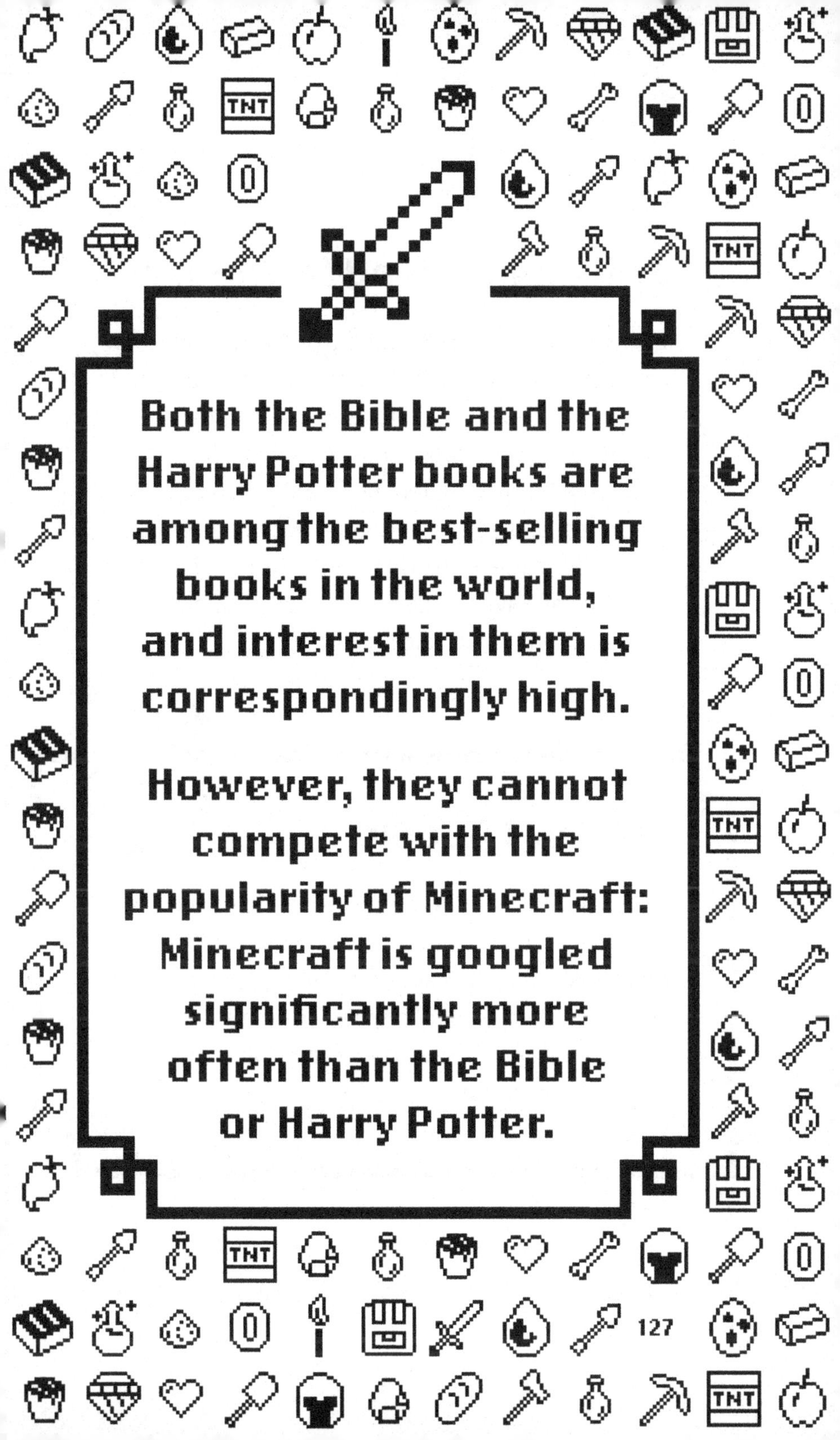

Both the Bible and the Harry Potter books are among the best-selling books in the world, and interest in them is correspondingly high.

However, they cannot compete with the popularity of Minecraft: Minecraft is googled significantly more often than the Bible or Harry Potter.

## Still on the Road to Victory

Even in its early years, *Minecraft* knew how to impress players and critics, winning one award after another. For example, the renowned games magazine *Rock, Paper, Shotgun* named *Minecraft* its Game of the Year in 2010 — and the full version hadn't even been released yet. More than a decade after its release, the game is still racking up awards, including the title of Favorite Game at the 2022 and 2023 Nickelodeon Kids' Choice Awards.

## Cute but Deadly

A truly funny sight: A Baby Zombie riding a chicken looks very funny at first. But if you don't make a hasty exit, these so-called Chicken Jockeys will make your life a living hell. They like to hop on the back of mounts and chase you — and sometimes that mount is a chicken.

## Red-Green Deficiency?

Rubies are used as currency in many video games, for example, including *The Legend of Zelda* series. *Minecraft* was about to follow suit, but developer Dinnerbone noticed something important: Ruby and Redstone Blocks are almost indistinguishable for people with color blindness — Dinnerbone himself is affected by this. As a result, rubies were replaced with emeralds at the very last minute, and since then you have been trading emeralds with Villagers — not rubies.

## Unusual Piglets

Along with Silverfish, Baby Hoglins are the weakest monsters in *Minecraft*. In the Easy and Normal difficulty levels, they will only take half a heart from you. A full-grown Hoglin on the other hand, can hurl you into the air like an Iron Golem. And if you attack a Hoglin of this type, all of its relatives in the vicinity will attack you. Strangely enough, if you attack one of their babies, the pack will not automatically attack you.

## Like Winning the Lottery

Do you know "Minceraft"? This spelling mistake, which happens when you type too fast — the E and the C are reversed — quickly became an inside joke. Notch made fun of it and incorporated it into the game: With a 1 in 10,000 chance, your home screen will alternatively say "Minceraft" instead of *Minecraft.* This Easter Egg initially remained undiscovered, and after Notch said in an interview that there was something else that no player had discovered, he was bombarded with screenshots and messages from eager discoverers. He then announced that he would never speak publicly about the "Minceraft" Easter Egg again.

## A Big Thank You

2011 was a good year for *Minecraft* and Mojang. Not only did the game reach record numbers, but at the end of the year, the game finally made it out of beta and reached full version status. To celebrate the year and thank his employees, Notch paid out around 2.7 million dollars in bonuses to a staff of around 20.

## A Work of Art

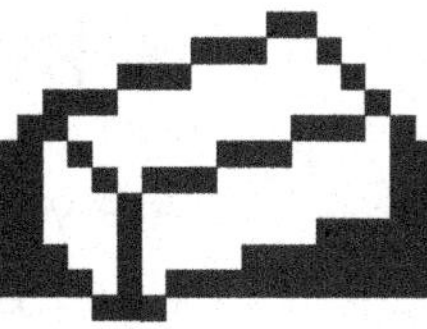

In 2017, the Newheaven collective was invited to collaborate with the renowned French design school Lisaa in Paris. To mark the occasion, the hard-working builders simply recreated perhaps the most famous museum in the world, the Louvre, in *Minecraft*. In total, 11 people spent around 40 days block-building for all they were worth. The result is so impressive that even the official *Minecraft* website reported on it.

## Hold Tight …

… when the Wither Storm arises! This monster is a final boss in *Minecraft Story Mode,* and with its three heads and huge tentacles it looks extremely terrifying. It was crafted by Ivor, a renegade of the Order of the Stone, making it the first villain to be created by a human. Although all of its ingredients are available in the normal game, it is not possible to craft a Wither Storm in *Minecraft*.

## X-Ray Vision

Are you in the middle of a fight and want to take cover behind a wall or sneak away? Unfortunately, it doesn't always work. Certain mobs can see you through walls. These include Slimes, Spiders, and the relatively harmless Silverfish. Illusioners — a type of Illagers that fight with magic and a bow — can also see through walls. But don't worry. These enemies do not occur naturally in *Minecraft.* Although they were added to the game code in version 1.12, they are not yet used officially.

### The Ravages of Time

For around 10 years, the *Minecraft Java Edition* launcher icon was the in-game Crafting Table icon. In the summer of 2023, this icon was replaced with the Grass Block icon, and the icons of the *Bedrock Edition* and the *Minecraft Launcher* also received minor graphic overhauls. According to Mojang, the new icons are more contemporary and easier to distinguish.

## Our Poem

According to his own statement, the author of the end-credits poem, Irish author Julian Gough (see page 17), had not signed a proper contract for his work on *Minecraft* — neither with Mojang Studios nor with Microsoft. Although he received a payment of around 20,000 dollars, the legal situation as to who was the rightful owner of the poem remained unclear. Deterred by a possible legal dispute with Microsoft and after careful consideration, Gough then announced in late 2022, a full 11 years after the poem had been incorporated into *Minecraft,* that he was placing the poem into the public domain. This means that the poem is license-free and can be accessed and used by anyone. Microsoft has not responded to this announcement.

## Waste Incineration

Drops are not indestructible: lava, cacti, explosions — everything that can be dangerous to you can also be a danger to drops. Well, almost everything. If you shoot at drops with arrows, for example, they will remain intact. So, if you want to dispose of items properly, we recommend building a lava pit or something similar.

## Block Speed

And how fast are you? Your character's normal walking speed in *Minecraft* is around 9.6 mph — that's 4.3 blocks per second. With the Soul Speed enchantment, you can reach a top speed of almost 20.5 mph, or nine blocks per second. However, you can reach the highest possible speed with the largest TNT cannon: 3,937,000 mph, which is the equivalent of 1,760,000 blocks per second.

## Not Quite So Secret

The Super Secret Settings were not really "super-secret," as this special menu was accessible via a simple button before it was removed from *Minecraft.* It allowed you to change the shader settings, i.e., the way the game world was displayed — a bit like a filter. Whether you wanted to see the world through the eyes of a Creeper or as if it were a work of art, the Super Secret Settings made it possible.

## Music in My Blocks

There are a total of 16 Music Disks in *Minecraft*, most of which can be found in Chests in various locations. However, there is also another way to get hold of the music. If you manage to get a Skeleton to kill a Creeper, it will drop a Music Disk. You can play the songs on the Jukebox. Incidentally, the slot in the Jukebox block always faces north or south — a very unusual compass.

## Notch's Word

The early days of *Minecraft's* development are well documented, as Markus Persson has recorded the history of the game's creation on his personal blog, *The Word of Notch.* The first entry dates back to May 13, 2009, and is, therefore, four days older than the first playable version of *Minecraft*. Notch wrote his last blog entry on August 19, 2013. As of today, the blog is offline and no longer accessible.

## When Worlds Collide

From *Ice Age* to *Sonic* to *Minions* — *Minecraft* has already collaborated with a number of well-known media universes. Most of these are limited to exclusive skins for your game character. But sometimes, you can also enter themed areas, such as a recreated Mushroom Kingdom in the *Super Mario* crossover on Nintendo Switch.

## Swung too Far

A cease-and-desist letter due to a misunderstanding? In July 2013, Mojang received a warning from the US mini-golf chain Putt-Putt. Enclosed were Google screenshots of videos showing putt-putt courses being recreated by players. Mojang's lawyer said that this could only be a misunderstanding. After all, Mojang cannot control what players build and film in *Minecraft*. He drew the following comparison: Microsoft cannot control what people write in Word or other text programs on their PCs either.

## No Risk, no Crown and Council

When the board game *Risk* meets *Minecraft*, the result is *Crown and Council*. Mojang employee Henrik Pettersson developed the turn-based strategy game single-handedly — just on the side. He himself described the project as an "experiment". *Crown and Council* is still available for free on platforms such as Steam and other download sites.

## Welcome to Minecraft Land

Ever wanted to recreate your garden in *Minecraft?* In Denmark, some civil servants had a similar idea in 2014 — only on a much bigger scale. Using an algorithm, they recreated the landscape of all of Denmark in *Minecraft*. Players could then admire the creation on a dedicated server and even expand it. Hard-working inventors were quick to recreate landmarks such as castles, but the first rioters were just as quick to demolish buildings. This was not a problem for the state employees, who considered destruction as part of the *Minecraft* game principle.

## The Hour of Code

Do you want to learn programming but don't know where to start? The *Minecraft* Hour of Code is the perfect place to start. In partnership with Code.org, which aims to offer students around the world the opportunity to learn programming for free, you can take part in a one-hour coding course. Using the familiar *Minecraft* environment, you will be taught the basics of programming. Since 2019, the *Minecraft Education* version has also been offering new courses every year.

## Before the Time of the Crown

Before Notch really took off with *Minecraft*, the Swede worked as a developer for several other companies. Between 2004 and 2009, he programmed browser games for the studios Midasplayer and King. Does that name sound familiar? No wonder, as King released a real long-running hit with *Candy Crush* in 2012. However, Notch has nothing to do with the smartphone game, having left the company three years earlier to focus on his own hit — *Minecraft.*

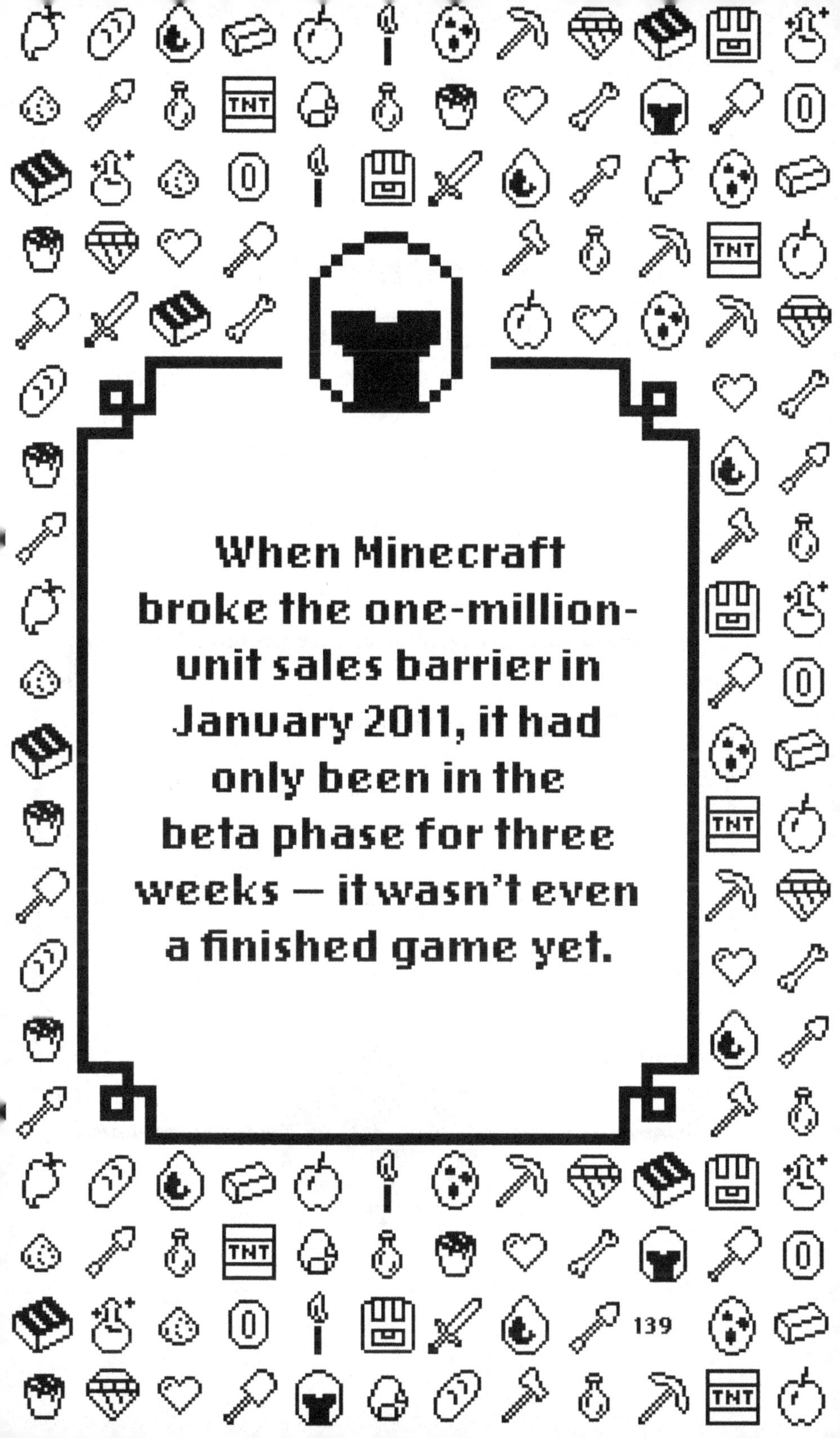

When Minecraft broke the one-million-unit sales barrier in January 2011, it had only been in the beta phase for three weeks — it wasn't even a finished game yet.

## Once Around the World

If your dream is to work at Mojang one day, you might have to prepare yourself for a move. The studio was founded in Stockholm, Sweden, and now has offices in Redmond, USA, as well as in China, Japan, and the UK. In total, around 600 people work at Mojang Studios — maybe one day it will be you?

## Drop or Dispense?

The Dispenser or Dropper Block looks like an oven, but it works slightly differently. As its name suggests, it ejects objects, making it ideal as a shot trap in combination with arrows, for example. Like a Chest, the Dropper or Dispenser has its own inventory. The objects dispensed are selected randomly, so there is no specific order in which they are ejected.

# Short & Sweet

Similar to the Ender Dragon, the Wither could also have a name. At least one Mojang employee responded to a question about the Wither's name in an official Youtube video with: "Simmons?"

Of all adult *Minecraft* players, around 41% are between the ages of 18 and 24 — with a respectable 3% of players over the age of 65.

Silverfish in the cave? Just like in real life, these little insects are hard to catch. Unlike most other creatures, Silverfish are constantly on the move.

Before the Hardcore Mode was officially introduced, a similar, self-imposed way of playing was popular in the *Minecraft* community. In this mode, you manually delete your savestate after dying — this is called "Ironman".

# Short & Sweet

Among the top 10 most-followed Twitch channels in the world, there are four streamers who are largely dedicated to *Minecraft.* This clearly speaks for the success of the game.

Getting lost in *Minecraft's* vast world is easier than you might think. That's why there are a few tricks to help you get your bearings. For example, you can place carved pumpkins so that their faces are facing towards your camp.

With 2.5 million downloads in just nine days, the launch of the *Minecraft Earth* augmented reality app in November 2019 looked great. However, less than two years later, Microsoft pulled the plug on development.

Over the Christmas holidays, the Chests in *Minecraft* will have a new look.

## Infinite Potential

In the past, it was common for a game to be complete when the full version was released and updates were no longer required. This was especially true in 2011, when the full version of *Minecraft* was released — but more than a decade later, *Minecraft* continues to receive new content on a regular basis. Notch explained this when he was still responsible for the game: *Minecraft* is simply a game with infinite potential, so Mojang should take advantage of that and keep improving and expanding the game.

## Not Pinocchio

With their long noses, the Villagers remind some players of Squidward from the animated series *Spongebob Squarepants*. However, it was the cult game *Dungeon Master 2* that served as a source of inspiration. When asked about the Villagers' appearance, Notch revealed on Reddit that they were based on the shopkeepers from *Dungeon Master 2* — rather than grumpy, clarinet-playing squids.

## Let the Party Begin

Canadian music producer Deadmau5 has always been a big fan of *Minecraft*. He has created his own Youtube videos on the subject and even wrote a song especially for the game. *Professional Griefers* is a collaboration with the singer of the band My Chemical Romance, Gerard Way, and was chosen as the theme song for the official *Minecraft* release. In 2012, Deadmau5 gave an exclusive concert at Minecon, during which he swapped his trademark mouse mask with huge ears for a Steve Head during the performance. He also attacked a *Minecraft* chicken figure with a *Minecraft* sword — a night to remember.

## Add It to the Playlist

Got a favorite *Minecraft* song? The soundtrack is extremely popular, and the catalog continues to grow with additional songs with each mash-up pack. You can also now officially listen to many songs on Spotify and other streaming platforms, as Microsoft is releasing more and more *Minecraft* albums. You can also listen to tracks composed by C418.

## The Golem in the Sky

Iron Golems protect villages and their inhabitants, sometimes even giving them poppies. This close relationship is reflected in their faces, as the golems bear a striking resemblance to the Villagers. However, their bodies are based on a completely different model: In the anime film *Castle in the Sky* by the celebrated Japanese animation company Studio Ghibli, there is a robot that protects the local flora and fauna — and even gives out flowers.

## Dance, Dance, Hoglin!

Hoglins and Piglins are not on friendly terms. Former Mojang developer Henrik Kniberg, who is credited with the creation of the Hoglins, posted a video on his private channel a month before the monsters were added to *Minecraft*. The video shows a group of Hoglins killing a Piglin and then celebrating this with a tactful head nod and a bipedal dance. However, this feature never made it into the game.

## Again No Publication

Even in his post-*Minecraft* days, Markus Persson still has a few fans. And when Notch published screenshots of a new game project in January 2018, nobody was surprised by the ensuing uproar. The images of the "Voxels_WebGL2" project are indeed somewhat reminiscent of *Minecraft*, thanks in part to the minimalist graphic style and expansive landscapes. However, a playable version never saw the light of day — as with most of Persson's projects.

## Sweat and Tears

Do you think Notch put his heart and soul into creating and developing *Minecraft*? A fan asked him this question on the platform X — and Notch replied in the negative. Although he had a lot of fun working on *Minecraft*, he said he didn't put his heart and soul into it. Nevertheless, he is now enjoying his retirement as a billionaire, although he admitted it can be a little boring.

## April Fool's Day

Notch likes to make jokes — as he did on April 1, 2012, when he announced his "new" space adventure, *Mars Effect,* and its website. Does the name sound familiar? In fact, there is a video game series called *Mass Effect.* With this play on words, Notch took a little jab at Bethesda, who had just sued Mojang. The reason for this was the title of the new *Scrolls* project, which was allegedly too similar to Bethesda's *The Elder Scrolls* series (see page 74). The fake announcement was actually supposed to result in Notch's new project *0x10c* — a space adventure — which never saw the light of day.

## Like the Lottery

The rarest mob in *Minecraft Bedrock Edition* is clearly a Desert Baby Zombie, wearing gear and armor and riding a brown baby panda. All of these things are very rare on their own. But the odds of them happening at the same time are about 1 in 3,472 trillion.

## Three Days Awake

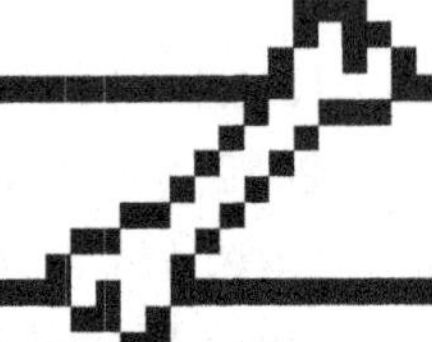

Just like in real life, sleep is extremely important because a sleep deficit can be dangerous. In *Minecraft,* this manifests itself in a unique way. If you haven't used a bed for three in-game days, Phantoms will appear. And they will hunt you down. Phantoms are ray-like flying monsters that can spawn up to five times a night — but they take damage in sunlight. Their packs consist of up to four monsters that circle above you like vultures. Well, good night ...

## Of Witches and Wizards

Very few creatures in *Minecraft* have a gender, and Witches are no exception. Although their name implies a female form, as a fan on the platform X pointed out, Mojang developer Dinnerbone has taken a stand, insisting that the term "witch" does not exclude the male form. This means that *Minecraft's* Witches are definitely genderless.

## Freedom of Expression

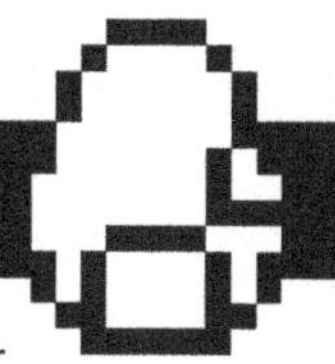

"A little bit dead" — this is how *Minecraft* creator Notch described the game in 2021 after a new skin DLC was announced. Although the sales and player numbers contradict his statement, Notch has his own opinion. Following the sale of his *Minecraft* brand to Microsoft, he has repeatedly spoken critically about the direction in which *Minecraft* has developed. In particular, he has repeatedly criticized paid micro-transactions.

### Until the End

Are you one of them? *Minecraft Dungeons* was released on May 26, 2020, and attracted around 11.5 million players in a span of one year. More than three years later, in September 2023, developer Mojang announced that more than 25 million players have now torn their way through the caves. However, Update 1.17 is still the final version. *Minecraft Dungeons* is now complete.

## Too Much Math

The maximum number of items you can carry in your inventory and in your hands is 37. If you now fill all the compartments with Shulker Boxes, each of which has 27 compartments filled with 64 stacks, you will be carrying an incredibly large number of blocks around with you. If you take an Ender Chest and fill its 27 compartments with Shulker Boxes, which in turn are overflowing with stacks, you will be carrying over 100,000 individual items. And the calculation goes on and on. Sit on a donkey that you load up with Shulker Boxes and pull llamas behind you, whose inventory you also fill ... Do you really need that much space?

## Put It in the Sound Mixer

Sneezing baby pandas are extremely cute. But they are also not so easy to record on sound. That's why the sound designers at Mojang came up with the trick of mixing the sounds of several animals. A baby panda's sneeze in *Minecraft* is made up of the sounds of a cat, a parrot imitating a sneeze and — of course — baby panda sounds.

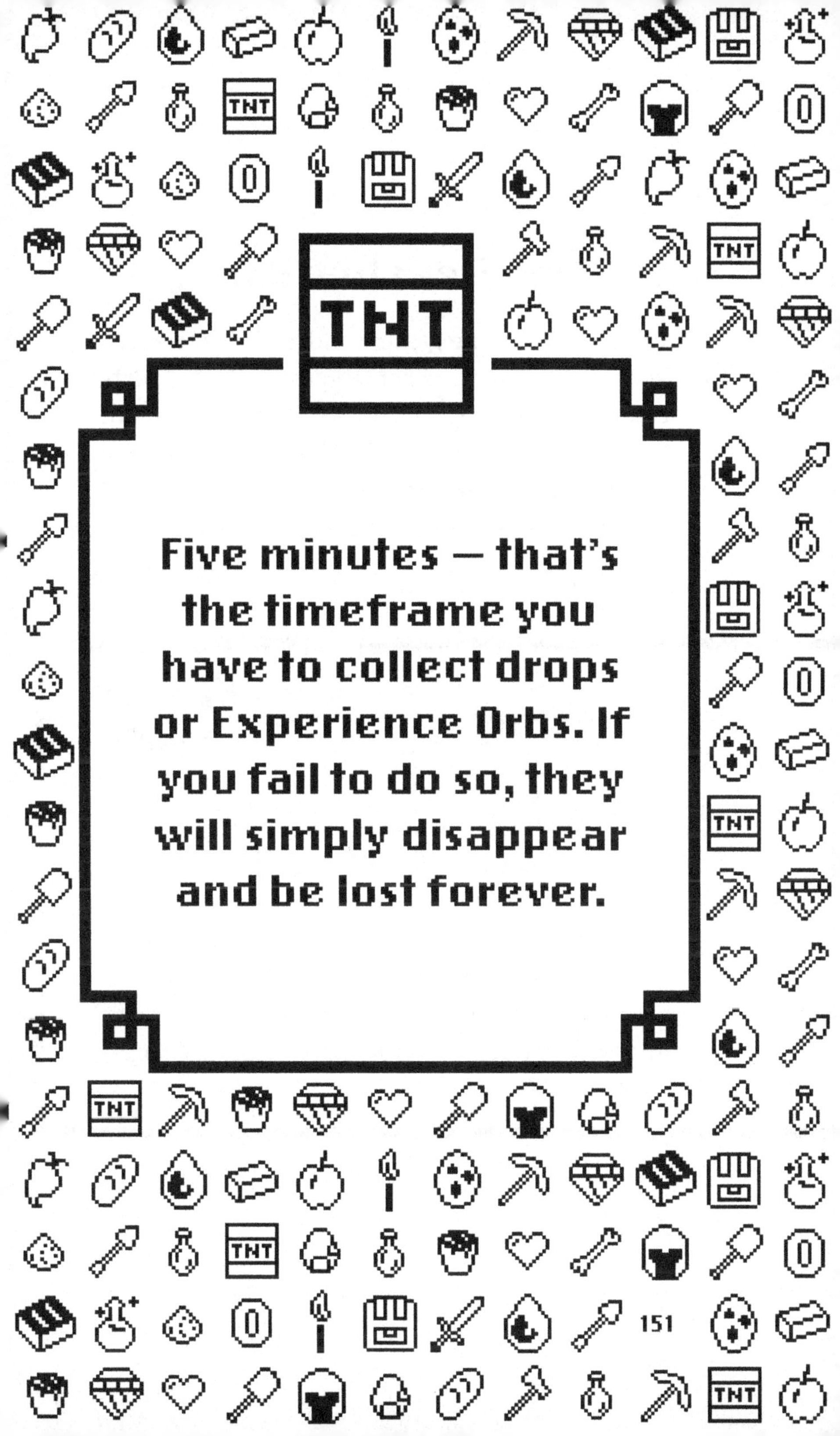
TNT
Five minutes — that's the timeframe you have to collect drops or Experience Orbs. If you fail to do so, they will simply disappear and be lost forever.

## Floating Trees that Burn

When pieces of the game world, so-called chunks, are created, trees are sometimes the first objects created. As a result, lakes can form underneath them — causing the trees to float. If, by chance, a lava lake is also created above ground, this can lead to a forest fire — with serious consequences.

## Live-Craft

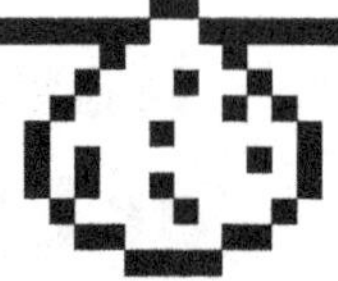

What does game programming actually look like? If you follow Notch on Twitch, you probably have an answer to that question. When he developed the game *Minicraft* for the Ludum Dare coding contest in December 2011, Notch streamed the development process live. For almost 25 hours, you were able to watch a game being made and gain a deep insight into Notch's way of programming. Pretty exciting!

# Short & Sweet

Desert Zombies are just withered Zombies, aren't they? Not quite. The undead from the Desert are actually a little bigger than normal Zombies.

Every year in October, Minecraft Live hosts a livestream. As well as celebrating the game, viewers can vote for new creatures to be added to the game in future updates.

In reality, cats almost always land on all four paws as a reflex to effectively cushion the fall. They can also survive greater heights without damage. This has been adopted in *Minecraft* to the extent that cats are immune to fall damage.

Do you know what a déjà vu is? In the game files for the yellow splash texts in the start menu, the entry "Déjà vu!" appears twice. Do you know what a déjà vu is?

## Short & Sweet

Notch's space adventure game *0x10c* was unfortunately never published, but the idea behind it is interesting. It is set 281,474,976,710,656 years (which corresponds to the number 0x10c in hexadecimal notation) after the year 1988.

In 2013, the renowned Time Magazine named Markus "Notch" Persson as the inventor and Jens "Jeb" Bergensten as the developer responsible for *Minecraft* among the 100 most influential people of the year.

Is your wolf healthy? The lower a wolf's tail is, the worse its health.

The original idea was for the villages to be inhabited by pig people. However, this idea was rejected, and the Villagers we know today moved in.

## How It All Began

Do you like documentaries? Then the movie *Minecraft — The Story of Mojang* is just right for you. It tells the story of *Minecraft* and the development studio behind it. When the documentary was released in late 2012, the production company 2 Player Productions even uploaded the film to popular piracy websites so that as many people as possible would have the chance to watch *Minecraft — The Story of Mojang.* The production company has nevertheless asked people to support the documentary through DVD or digital purchases.

## From Bug to Feature

Former Mojang developer Tommaso Checchi accidentally removed the bottom layer of villages, which checks whether the terrain is suitable for villages. The result was that the settlements were created on water — and somehow that went down well. Checchi simply replaced the footpaths with wooden planks, and since then, villages can also be built on water.

## It Doesn't Always Have to Be Digital

You can also play *Minecraft* analogously. If you want to ditch the controller or mouse and keyboard and still dive into the block adventure, there are plenty of options. In addition to *Minecraft* Lego sets, there are also some board games in *Minecraft* design, including the popular card game *Uno*.

## Many Registrations, Few Sales

Eight months after its initial release in January 2010, *Minecraft* reached a milestone: the 100,000th player registered on the official website. To celebrate, he or she received a special congratulatory message and a free copy of *Minecraft*. How generous! At that point, however, the number of copies of the game sold was significantly lower, as only around 3,600 of these registered users actually bought *Minecraft* — that's less than four percent of users.

## A Scary Company

In the early 2010s, it wasn't just *Minecraft* that was experiencing a huge hype. Virtual reality was on everyone's lips. So, it made sense that Mojang was also planning a VR version of *Minecraft.* But when Oculus, the market leader in VR goggles at the time, was finally bought by Facebook in 2013, Notch scrapped the VR plans. By his own admission, he did not trust Facebook and simply found the company scary. However, after Microsoft took over responsibility for the *Minecraft* brand, the first official VR version of the game was released in 2016.

## How Many Calories Is That?

Are you strong enough? In reality, pure gold weighs about 19 grams per cubic centimeter. Translated to a Block of Gold in *Minecraft*, it would weigh about 19 tons. In the game, one Block of Gold can be used to craft nine Gold Ingots, each weighing around two tons. If you were to craft a Golden Apple, which requires eight Gold Ingots and one Apple, it would actually weigh just over 17 tons.

## Dungeons and Ender Dragons

As a popular brand, *Minecraft* has had its fair share of collaborations. Nerds who not only enjoy digital adventures but also like to play analog, tabletop role-playing games such as *Dungeons and Dragons* were treated to two very special mash-up expansions in spring 2023. Not only has an official *Dungeons and Dragons* DLC been released for *Minecraft*, immersing you in a world full of goblins and dice. Mojang and D&D Beyond have also created an official and free version of the Monstrous Compendium that will allow you to add the following five mobs to your next *Dungeons and Dragons* session: the Creeper, the Blaze, the Ender Dragon, the Enderman, and the Wolf.

## A Huge Circle of Friends

One of 19 million? If you play on the Hypixel server, you are part of the largest *Minecraft* server in the world. The network holds four official Guinness World Records, including the one for the most game modes (43) on one server. You can join the server, which is available in 24 languages, via the *Java* version of *Minecraft*.

## It's Not About Graphics

When you hear *Minecraft 4k*, do you think of 4K graphics performance? Think again. *Minecraft 4k* is a minimalist version of the game that Notch created for a programming competition. The aim was to program a game that was no larger than 4 kilobytes. *Minecraft 4k* has a size of 2.52 kilobytes and was released on December 2, 2009. For comparison, the downloadable version of *Minecraft* for PC is over 1 gigabyte, almost 400,000 times the size of *Minecraft 4k*. In this minimalist version, the size of the game world is 64 by 64 by 64 blocks — not much room to let off steam.

## Unnecessary Block?

One game element that Notch regrets having included in *Minecraft* is the Slab. After all, the size of a block has a purpose, and the game was designed for whole blocks, not half blocks. Especially now that Stairs have found their way into the game, Notch says that Slabs have become completely unnecessary. Do you agree or disagree with him?

## Please Do Not Try This at Home

Do you find *Minecraft* immersive? For Youtubers Dream and Georgenotfound, the game can't get real enough. The two have modified an electronic dog collar to deliver a small shock when the player suffers damage in *Minecraft.* The video of this crazy experiment has already been viewed more than 38 million times — imitation is not recommended!

## Another Guest Appearance

The indie game *Super Meat Boy* is not only known for its fun factor but is also notorious for its level of difficulty. In the Steam version of the game, you can unlock a special character: Mr. Minecraft. This is, of course, none other than Steve. Although Steve can't jump as high as other characters in *Super Meat Boy,* he can build platforms. Pretty handy for such a challenging game.

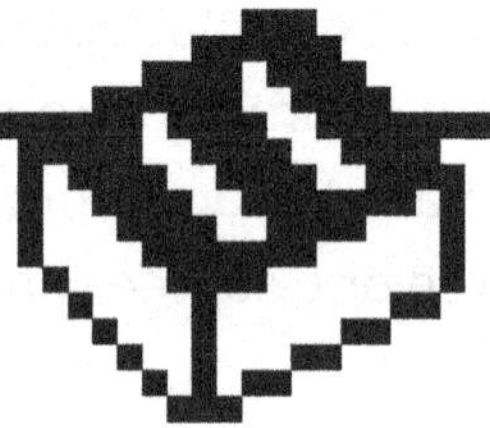

## Noise Without Feet

Despite not having feet, some mobs make the sound of footsteps. These include floating monsters such as the Wither or the Blaze, as well as aquatic animals such as dolphins and salmon. In the past, Ghasts and Phantoms also made these stomping noises, but this bug has since been patched out of the game.

## Lots of Colorful Rainbow Sheep

Do you like it colorful? Then you should name one of your sheep "jeb_" using an anvil or a name tag. As a result, this sheep will constantly change its wool color. Unfortunately, it will change back to its original color when you shear or kill it. The name "jeb_" is the in-game name of the lead developer Jens "Jeb" Bergensten. A nice Easter Egg.

## Eyes Open at Night

Have you ever seen a fox attacking its prey in *Minecraft*? It does this by leaping into the air and pouncing on its prey. This behavior is not a figment of your imagination but based on the hunting behavior of real foxes. In theory, *Minecraft's* cunning hunters can also jump over fences and walls. But since they can't even see through fences, they don't usually attack chickens behind them. The fact that you can encounter foxes in villages at night is also due to the behavior of real foxes, who like to explore dark streets in the real world.

## Almost Like Before

Arcade machines in the 21st century? They really do exist — and *Minecraft Dungeons* is one of the games you can play on one. The first machines were delivered to arcades in May 2021. With up to three friends, you can slash your way through nine levels and even modify your equipment with special collectible cards. Have you spotted a *Minecraft Dungeons* arcade machine in real life?

## So Much Boredom

When Notch sold *Minecraft* to Microsoft in 2014, he left Mojang a billionaire. But such a life does not seem to be entirely fulfilling. That's why Notch set up a company called Rubberbrain to develop new games. And although he has already invested over five million euros in production, not a single project has been published to date.

## A Curious Piece of Minecraft History

If you were using a smartphone between 2011 and 2014, you could download and play *Minecraft Pocket Edition Lite.* In this demo version, the overall gaming experience was quite limited — you couldn't even save your game and had to start your building projects from scratch every time you started. You also couldn't name your character. Instead, you were automatically given the name "Stevie" — not Steve, mind you.

## All Good Things Come in Twos — or Maybe Not

Would you like to see a *Minecraft* sequel? Those responsible at Mojang and Microsoft tend to disagree: *Minecraft 2* wouldn't be a good idea. The risk of dividing the community is simply too great. And as long as the original is still so successful, there is no need for a sequel. But never say never ...

## Grass and Its Relatives

In most biomes — at least those in the Overworld — the Grass Block is one of the most important foundations. No wonder, as the Grass Block is one of the most commonly used blocks in *Minecraft*. However, there are only a few biomes where other blocks dominate. This is the case in Mushroom Fields, for example, where the Mycelium Block has the same function as grass but replaces it. After all, the mushrooms simply thrive best on these blocks. Podzol, on the other hand, is low in nutrients and, unlike Mycelium Blocks, cannot be transferred to other blocks. You can find this type of soil in the Bamboo Jungle and Old Growth Taiga biomes.

# Short & Sweet

If you use a bed in the Nether or the End, it will explode — but if a Villager uses it, there will be no explosion if it is nighttime in the Overworld. Instead, the Villager can take a peaceful nap.

As you know, the creepy character Herobrine is pure fantasy and doesn't really exist in *Minecraft*. Despite this, game update messages often state that Herobrine has been removed from the game — an obvious joke ... right?

Steve's face was inspired by the character from the 90s shooter *Quake*.

When a turtle is struck by lightning in the *Java Edition* — whether from a thunderstorm or a trident — it will occasionally drop a bowl. This is a reference to the shape of the turtle's shell.

# Short & Sweet

Some creatures in *Minecraft* have personal names — such as the game characters Steve and Alex, or Jean the Ender Dragon. The particularly fierce Wardens also have such names. "Jonathan" and "William" are both in use.

Snow and rain fall from the clouds — at least in the real world. Not so in *Minecraft*, where both weather phenomena somehow originate above the clouds and simply fall through them.

What is a Netherrack actually made of? *Minecraft Education* has the answer. The stone from the Nether consists of 64% silicon, 18% oxygen, 15% mercury — and the remaining 3% is undetermined since the substance has not yet been discovered.

## Almost Changed Jobs

Would you have said no? In August 2010, Notch was invited to Seattle for an interview by Valve, the company behind the platform Steam and games such as *Portal.* He was offered a job at Valve but declined. Instead of seeing *Minecraft* on Steam, he wanted to build his own Valve — which he eventually did with Mojang.

## All the Best

For a few years, if you started *Minecraft* on November 9, you could read the splash text "Happy birthday, ez!" in the main menu. This was a salute to Notch's former partner, who celebrates her birthday on that day. And although they divorced back in 2012, the message was only removed in May 2015 — around six months after Notch left Mojang for good.

## A New Home

After Notch became a billionaire thanks to the Microsoft acquisition of *Minecraft*, he left his home in Sweden and moved to Beverly Hills. He bought a mansion there for around 70 million dollars. This made waves not only because of the record price but also because Persson outbid the two superstars Beyoncé and Jay-Z when buying the house.

## Where Are the Udders?

When Jeb started working on *Minecraft,* the first creatures he created were squids. He did this by copying and adapting the cow model. This made it possible to milk squids for a while. It was only after a year that he corrected the error and promptly received messages about how unfortunate this change was. After all, who wouldn't want to drink squid milk?

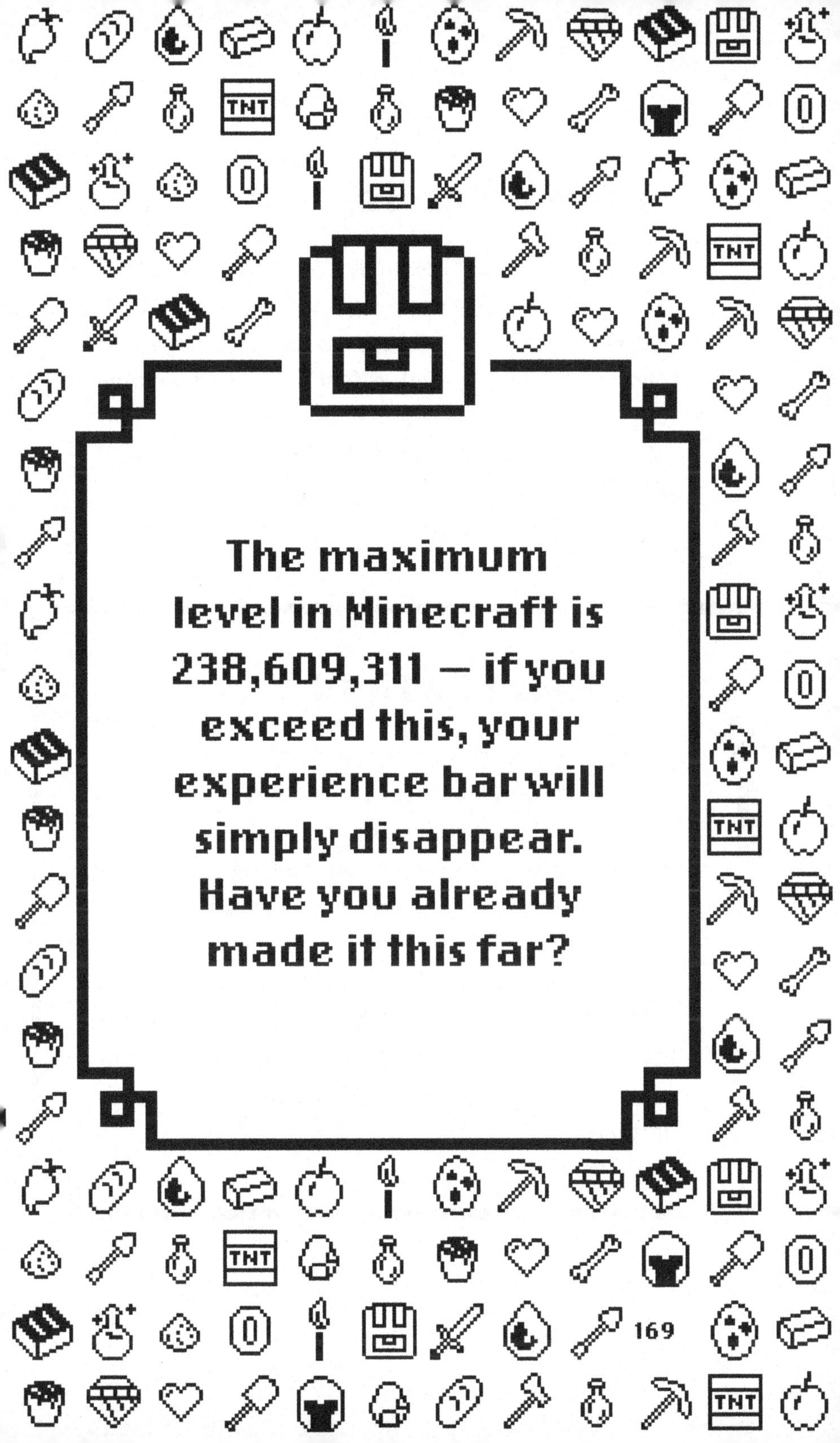

The maximum level in Minecraft is 238,609,311 — if you exceed this, your experience bar will simply disappear. Have you already made it this far?

## Just like Before

The name "Wither" actually comes from another game. *Whispers in Akarra* is the video game that Jeb worked on before he became lead developer on *Minecraft* (see page 94). It features a poison spell called "Wither" — and apparently, it reminded him of the boss monster. How fitting, as the Wither is also an undead creature.

## Let There Be Light

When frogs come into contact with small Magma Cubes, the monsters turn into lamps. These so-called Froglights shine brighter than almost any other light source in *Minecraft*. Mojang considered adding fireflies to the game, which would turn into Froglight Blocks in the same way. In reality, however, some types of fireflies are poisonous to frogs, so the idea was scrapped. To date, fireflies have not made it into the game, although at just two pixels in size, they would probably be the smallest creatures in *Minecraft*.

## The Women in Notch's Life

From *Minecraft* forum moderator to ex-wife — Elin Zetterstrand has taken on extraordinary roles in Notch's life. However, the couple separated after just one year of marriage. Their daughter has three first names, one of which is Zelda. Yes, just like the princess from Nintendo's legendary game series.

## Don't Want to Share?

Many PC gamers use the platform Steam to buy and manage their PC games. Most major titles can be purchased there, including *Minecraft Legends* and *Minecraft Dungeons* — but not the original game. Jeb mentioned a few years ago that this would require a double login — to Steam and to Mojang — but since the release of the *Bedrock Edition* and the console port, the double login should no longer be an obstacle. Instead, there is speculation about another cause: For every game sold, Steam claims 20 to 25% of the revenue for itself — and Microsoft can do without this split for a game as successful as the original *Minecraft.* After all, the title is selling like hotcakes, even without being available on the Steam platform.

## Thanks to the Collective

*Minecraft* truly thrives on its community — and that needs to be celebrated. That's why Mojang launched the so-called Community Celebration in December 2020. For one month, you could download four player-created maps, as well as some Skins and other cosmetic items. Mojang wanted to express its gratitude to the *Minecraft* community.

## Advantages and Disadvantages

Thanks to *Minecraft,* a game model has become the industry standard that not everyone is comfortable with: Early Access. This means buying a game that is still in an alpha or beta phase, i.e. not yet fully developed. *Minecraft* sold millions of copies before the release of its full version, providing Mojang with funding that would not have been possible without Early Access. However, there is a downside to this practice. Numerous developers have offered Early Access versions of their games in subsequent years — but have failed to deliver full versions or have even gone underground with the money. This is why many gamers are critical of this model.

## Rich and Blocked

In the early days of *Minecraft*, when the full version was not yet available, and the hype around the game was just getting started, Notch's account was suspended by Paypal. The reason given: This unusually high flow of money could only have a criminal background. In reality, *Minecraft* was selling almost by the second, and millions of euros found their way into Persson's account.

0

## Which Came First — the Hen or the Duck?

One month before the release of the full version of *Minecraft,* Notch caused a stir with a statement that sent old fans into a rage: Chickens are now ducks. Even weeks later, Jeb had to keep correcting him — Notch was only joking. More than a decade later, the mood has probably changed a bit, and more and more players would like to see ducks in *Minecraft.* At least *Minecraft Dungeons* players can unlock a small pet duck to console themselves.

## No Desire for Wet Feathers

In the *Bedrock Edition,* parrots behave a little differently than in the *Java Edition*. For example, they will start dancing while sitting on your shoulder when a Music Disk is playing. Also, they will only jump off you if your shoulders come into contact with water — not if your feet get wet, as is the case in the *Java Edition.*

## Not in Love

As you know, Wardens are among the most dangerous creatures in *Minecraft*. To make you even more aware of this fact, there was an idea to display the player's heartbeat as they approached. However, there were concerns that this would be too much of a break in style. So, the Mojang developers came up with the idea to simply give the Wardens a clearly audible heartbeat.

## The Pewdiepie Effect

In the early 2010s, *Minecraft* and Let's Play videos were booming. Despite its success, streamer Pewdiepie was hardly producing any *Minecraft* content at the time, as he thought many were only doing so because of the game's popularity. Pewdiepie felt that only a few creators really enjoyed the game. A few years later, in the summer of 2019, he at least rediscovered his enjoyment of *Minecraft.* He regularly uploaded videos of his blocky adventures and promptly propelled the game back to the top of the Youtube charts. As a result, not only did other Youtubers jump on the renewed *Minecraft* bandwagon, but many players also reinstalled the game and for the first time in two years, the term "Minecraft" was typed in more often in the Youtube search bar than "Fortnite".

## Steven Block-Spielberg

Ever wanted to create your own *Minecraft* animated film? No problem at all! The Mine-imator program makes it possible. You can use it to create scenes, move characters, and even add all kinds of effects. In the end, you can upload your creation to Youtube. And action!

## Nothing but Empty Promises

Even before the Ender Dragon was added to the game via an update, Notch — who was still responsible for the game at the time — announced that there would be a peaceful dragon for the Overworld. It would be red and the same size as the Ender Dragon.

Two months later, Jeb was put in charge of the project and was now faced with a huge problem: How to fit a creature of that size into *Minecraft*? Especially since it was promised that this red dragon — unlike the Ender Dragon — would not destroy any blocks. An almost impossible task when you consider such complex biomes like the Jungle or the Mountain Grove. How would a gigantic dragon fly through them undisturbed?

In the early months, Jeb and his team were relatively optimistic that they would still be able to deliver the red dragon. Two years later, Notch himself stepped in and confirmed when asked: "It never happened." And so it was never meant to happen.

## Protect the Axolotl

Axolotls in *Minecraft* can have one of five colors: brown, pink, turquoise, gold, and blue. The latter is the rarest color variant. The chance of an axolotl being blue is 1 in 1,200, although this number is not chosen at random. In the real world, there are only about 1,200 of these special amphibians left in the wild. Therefore, they are considered to be highly endangered.

## Minecraft – Almost an EA Franchise?

*Minecraft's* success attracted the interest of large companies early on. Even before Microsoft struck and took over the brand in 2014, former EA CEO John Riccitiello visited Mojang Studios in early 2011. A takeover never materialized, however, as no serious offer was ever made. Notch made it clear that *Minecraft* was not for sale — or at least that was the status quo in 2011. Just three years later, he had apparently changed his mind.

## Record after Record

Youtuber Dream has held two Guinness World Records since June 2022. Firstly, his channel is the most subscribed channel dedicated to *Minecraft* on Youtube, with (at the time) over 29 million subscribers. Secondly, no other pure *Minecraft* gameplay video has as many clicks as *Minecraft Speedrunner VS 3 Hunters Grand Finale,* with over 114 million views (also at the time). Since then, both subscriptions and clicks have continued to rise. What will be the next record?

## What Does the Fox Say?

Some animal sounds, such as those of the dolphin and panda, have been specially recorded by the sound design team (see page 5). Unfortunately, this does not work for all animals, including the fox. Its calls in *Minecraft* are actually the superimposed sounds of cats and dogs. A little editing and bang — the fox calls are ready.

# Short & Sweet

Game errors crop up all the time during development. When frogs were added to *Minecraft,* they initially had an unusual behavior: They could eat goats.

If you use special sound programs to open and visualize the music on Music Disc 11, you can recognize a face in the spectrogram in the last 10 seconds of the song. Some players like to see this as proof of the existence of Herobrine, but the face can also be interpreted as an Enderman or a Creeper.

*Minecraft Legends* took just nine days in April 2023 to reach the three million player mark.

If you kill an (innocent) lamb, it will never drop anything. Yet, you will receive up to seven experience points when a lamb spawns.

# Short & Sweet

You can use a Brewing Stand to create potions and rescue Villagers from igloo basements, for example. However, to prevent you from using it too early in the game, the *Minecraft* developers have introduced the Blaze Powder fuel, which you must first obtain in the Nether.

To celebrate the milestone of 10 million *Minecraft* games sold in April 2013, Jeb announced a new game content that many players had been eagerly anticipating: Horses. He even enlisted the help of modder Drzhark, who had already successfully implemented a horse in *Minecraft* as a modification.

I see something you don't: Invisibility potions can disguise creatures. However, this only works to a limited extent with the Shulker. Only the outer husk of the shell-like monster becomes invisible, leaving the creature inside completely naked.

## Blocky Cartoon

Did you know that there is an animated series based on *Minecraft*? *Minecraft Mini Series* tells the story of a group of friends fighting to survive on islands. The storyline is similar to the one you play with your friends in *Minecraft.* The series was produced by Mojang and Xbox Game Studios in collaboration with toy company Mattel and animation studio Atomic Cartoons, and it was released on Youtube. Unfortunately, the episodes have not been received with enthusiasm by all viewers, so you have to make do with 16 episodes over two seasons. It doesn't help that each episode is only about five minutes long. What do you think of *Minecraft Mini Series*?

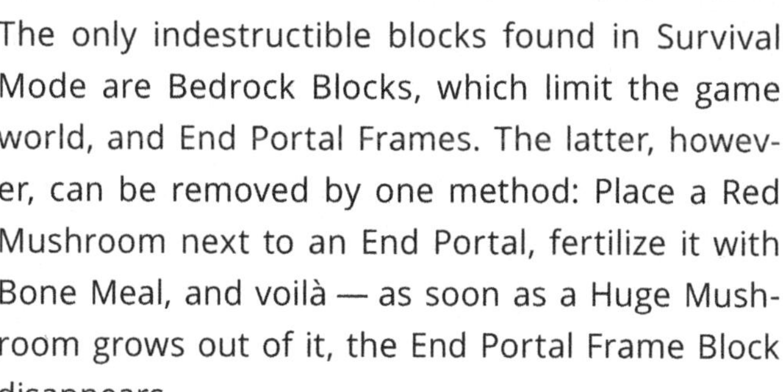

## Almost Indestructible

The only indestructible blocks found in Survival Mode are Bedrock Blocks, which limit the game world, and End Portal Frames. The latter, however, can be removed by one method: Place a Red Mushroom next to an End Portal, fertilize it with Bone Meal, and voilà — as soon as a Huge Mushroom grows out of it, the End Portal Frame Block disappears.

## Do You Speak Endermen-ish?

You've probably heard it before: Endermen sounds are simply phrases played backwards in English. But is it really true? There are several videos on the internet that claim to provide proof. However, *Minecraft's* sound designers have revealed in an official video that this is mostly speculation and that the majority of Endermen sounds are simply gibberish.

## Same but Different

At Mojang, it is customary to hold game jams after major updates. At these events, the developers are allowed to live out their wildest fantasies and program whatever they like. And so, it was at a game jam that developer Jason Major created a Desert Zombie. Jeb loved the idea, as he had already been planning to add more variety to the range of monsters. It was only logical that the Desert Zombie would find its way into the game.

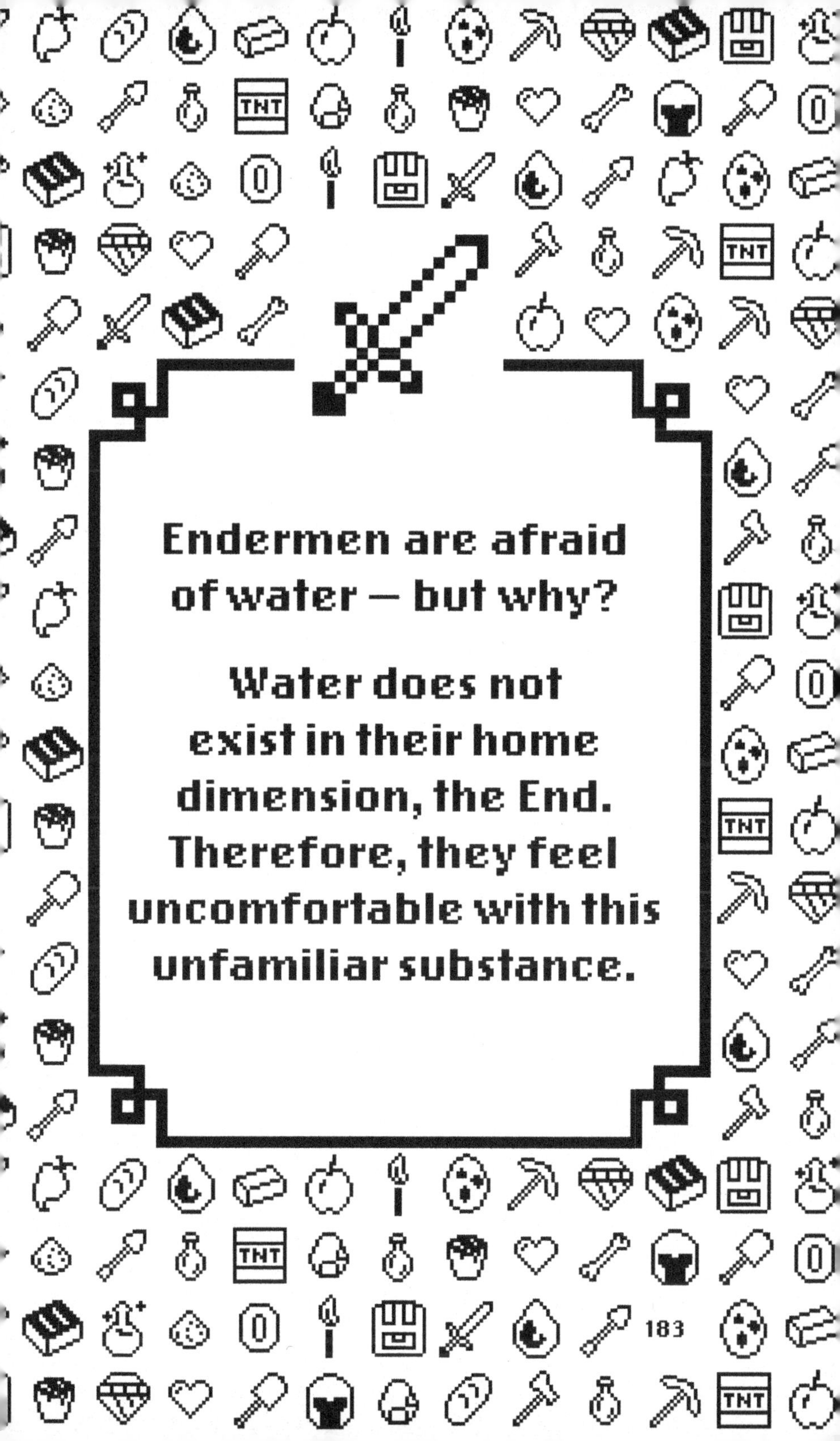

Endermen are afraid of water — but why?

Water does not exist in their home dimension, the End. Therefore, they feel uncomfortable with this unfamiliar substance.

Made in the USA
Las Vegas, NV
11 December 2024

13884674R00105